CEO PRINCIPLE$

GLOBAL
PUBLISHING
G R O U P

Global Publishing Group
Australia • New Zealand • Singapore • America • London

CEO PRINCIPLE$

How to Exponentially Grow Your Profits Through

AUTHENTIC LEADERSHIP

Foreword by
David Pich, CEO

AIM Australian Institute of Management

WORLD POSITIVITY LEADERS

WALT DISNEP

Dr John McIntosh & Elizabeth McIntosh

First Edition 2017

National Library of Australia
Cataloguing-in-Publication entry:

Creator: McIntosh, John H. (Harold John), 1960- author.

Title: CEO Principles : How To Exponentially Grow Your Profits Through Authentic Leadership / John Mcintosh ; Elizabeth McIntosh.

1st ed.
ISBN: 9781925288490 (paperback)

Success in business.
Leadership.
Employee motivation.
Customer service.

Other Creators/Contributors: McIntosh, Elizabeth M. (Elizabeth Mary-Rae), 1965- author.

Published by Global Publishing Group
PO Box 517 Mt Evelyn, Victoria 3796 Australia
Email info@GlobalPublishingGroup.com.au

For further information about orders:
Phone: +61 3 9726 4133 or Fax +61 3 8648 6871

This book is dedicated to all entrepreneurs, business owners, leaders, managers and supervisors who aspire to be greater than what they are today and have the courage to reach for the stars. It will be your leadership and inspiration that will create better employees, workplaces, communities and ultimately a better world.

Dr John McIntosh & Rev Elizabeth McIntosh

Acknowledgements

This book is a culmination of many years of business experience that has been made possible for us with many masters, teachers and coaches who imparted their wisdom unselfishly. The valuable life lessons and business insights have come from all sides and we thank every single one of them.

We would like to thank all of our staff and co-workers who supported us through the development and refinement of the business processes to create a phenomenal team and a fantastic business for everyone involved. Success in business is always dependent on having fantastic people around you with fantastic attitudes – congratulations to you all!

We would like to thank David Pich, CEO of Australian Institute of Management (AIM) for your support and encouragement in the process. AIM continues to provide excellence in management and leadership training, creating model future leaders. It is an honour to have been supported by AIM over the years and in the creation of this book.

A huge thanks to our publisher Global Publishing Group with Darren Stephens at the helm and his awesome team for their great work and dedication to the book's success. The wisdom that you have all imparted is priceless.

Any finally we want to thank all the participants in our seminars, workshops and research over the past years that shared their struggles and triumphs with us. Your heroic efforts to create change in your thinking and workplaces and the profound benefits that have occurred, made the writing of this book essential so these processes can be taken up globally. Thank you for being model leaders with the vision, passion and purpose that the world so desperately needs.

Our appreciation also goes out to our children for their support, encouragement and belief in us. They are an ongoing source of inspiration as they are already creating their own unique success pathways.

And last, but by no means least, the most amazing, brilliant, generous and considerate partner that each of us have ever had the pleasure of meeting, we thank each other!

John and Elizabeth

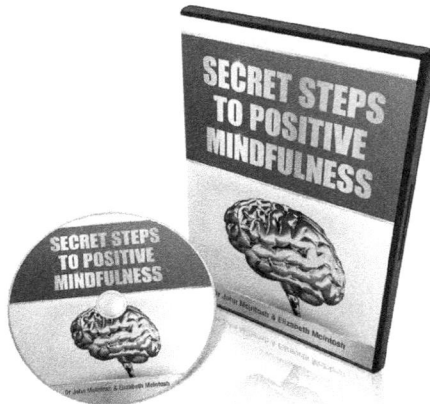

Contents

Foreword   **1**

Introduction   **3**

1. **How to Create a Positive Work Culture**   **7**

2. **Accentuate the Positive, Eliminate the Negative – at Work!**   **23**

3. **Five Steps to Positively Manage Mistakes**   **43**

4. **Positively Resolving Complaints, Conflict and Aggression**   **57**

5. **The 'Business Tree' Analogy**   **73**

6. **How to Hire and Retain Fantastic Staff**   **83**

7. **Ten Psychological Tips for Outstanding Customer Service**   **103**

8. **Toolbox of Positive Techniques**   **117**

9. **Positive Leadership Secrets**   **131**

10. **Four Steps to Achieving a Positive Bottom Line**   **151**

11. **How World Leaders use Positivity for Phenomenal Success**   **165**

Epilogue   **181**

About the Authors   **183**

Resources   **187**

Foreword

The Australian Institute of Management (AIM) believes passionately in sound management and leadership practice. At AIM we strive to remain at the cutting edge of developments in the leadership space, and there is no doubt that many of these developments are taking place in the area of mental health and mentally healthy workplaces.

Creating healthy workplace environments, with positive cultures and effective staff interactions is absolutely critical to business success. From a simple financial cost perspective alone, mental health impacts Australian businesses to the tune of $33 billion every year and is now the second most common claim under WorkCover.

The onus is increasingly on organisations to create positive, supportive workplaces – and to have effective strategies to assess and protect staff from mental health illness.

CEO Principles is an excellent reference point for organisations and for leaders. It provides strategies that are both practical and potentially extremely effective. It offers the reader new ways of recognising – and eliminating – negative thoughts and it suggests strategies for staff and colleagues to interact with each other in a positive and supportive way.

Crucially, the ideas presented by Dr John McIntosh & Rev Elizabeth McIntosh are based on creative ways to tackle the problems, mistakes and challenges that invariably occur in everyday business without drama or personal attacks.

Few people would argue that the potential to eliminate gossip, sarcasm and denigration from the workplace is not an exciting prospect!

CEO Principles is an exciting and refreshing read. The benefits of 'the principles' are clear – employees feels better, customers get better service and the business bottom line is dramatically improved! As such, this book offers the prospect of the elusive 'win, win, win'.

It's a must-read for everyone in business.

David Pich
Chief Executive
Australian Institute of Management

Introduction

Why the book "CEO *Principles*" was created

Imagine it was possible to create your workplace that was so happy and supportive that you could feel it as you walked in. Imagine what it would be like if your fellow workers were all friendly and positive, helping you to achieve the best you can do and all working together towards positive results in your business. Imagine if there was no sarcasm, backbiting, denigration, division or undermining. Imagine how it would feel if mistakes were treated as learning experiences for improvement and avoiding personal attacks. Imagine if the culture of the business was established to be positive and supportive and every staff member was held with value and integrity.

Imagine what it would be like if the atmosphere at your business was so pleasant that you looked forward to going to work and you knew that every day would be exciting and rewarding. Is that the sort of workplace you would like to work in?

Also imagine if, as a manager or owner, you had the tools to establish performance parameters from your staff that made them bound to achieve and legally accountable for compliance. Imagine if the stress of dealing with inter-personal conflict and staff issues were almost non-existent as systems were in place that were self-managing and self-auditing.

This book has the key steps to achieve all of the above!

It is possible to achieve this positive atmosphere and high-functioning staff and these new techniques are proven to be effective in real businesses and confirmed with research.

The rewards are outstanding. The outcomes from using these systems include:

- Improved staff productivity
- Improved staff retention
- Improved staff resilience and coping ability
- Reduced staff stress and reduced mental illness
- Improved customer service
- Improved customer loyalty (because they will enjoy the experience)
- Reduced staff conflict
- Reduced absenteeism
- Reduced risk of work place legal claims (unfair dismissal, harassment, stress leave)
- Dramatically improved bottom line

Not only will this process improve the workplace atmosphere and profitability, the benefits will also transform everyone's life outside of work, especially in personal and family relationships. Life skills will be developed to improved relationships with partners and children, perform better at other activities and take advantage of opportunities that arise. Everyone will benefit, both inside and outside the business as the positivity principles work their magic in all areas of life.

The principles of positive thinking have been well recognised for many years. However, this is the first time that effective strategies have been developed to recognise and eliminate negative thoughts. *CEO Principles* provides powerful strategies to catapult your business and staff to better outcomes, emotionally and financially. Until negative thoughts are recognised and controlled, they will sabotage and undermine everyone's success and happiness.

Creating a positive work environment requires buy-in at all levels of the business. Strategies are presented in the book to achieve this working from the vision and culture statements to the everyday interpersonal interactions. Self-monitoring techniques are also available so that the new positive atmosphere becomes the status quo and is maintained.

Our systems also offer processes to monitor and measure the staff and business atmosphere, mood, resilience and this has the ability to recognise staff members that require extra assistance to avoid sick days, stress leave or possibly even more severe mental illness. Our medical experience in mental illness allows us to offer this unique service that can save lives as well as money. Early prevention is always the best option.

Negative thoughts are like an unrecognised epidemic that is entrenched in most people's minds and they are often not even aware of it. Unfortunately, this often has crippling results in their physical, psychological and business achievements.

Research shows that up to 70% of visits to family doctors arise out of negative thoughts and attitudes. Plus, studies prove that you will live nine years longer if you have a positive outlook on life. It has also been shown that this optimistic approach to life results in less heart attacks, strokes, cancers and common colds! Therefore, this is not a nebulous and fluffy subject; it is critically important for the health and wellbeing of every single one of us personally and for our businesses.

We know that these systems work because we have instituted these principles in our multimillion dollar businesses around the world. We have bought businesses that had severely toxic atmospheres and instituted these principles with dramatic improvements in every way. The systems are effective in any industry and in any country and have been used effectively around the world.

As you read this book, you will have many "Ah-hah!" moments when you are hit with new realisations and moments of enlightenment. While it will have dramatic benefits to your business and workplace, negative thinking does affect every one of us personally, as well as our families, every day. Prepare to be amazed – you have been warned!

The ancient Eastern philosophers understood the power of thought. As Lao Tzu, the Buddhist leader, said:

> "Watch your thoughts; they become words.
> Watch your words; they become actions.
> Watch your actions; they become habits.
> Watch your habits; they become character.
> Watch your character; it becomes your destiny!"
> Let your journey to the bright side begin…

CHAPTER 1

How to Create a Positive Work Culture

CHAPTER 1

How to Create a Positive Work Culture

"Truly successful businesses are not just about making money, but positively changing the world for the greater good."

— Eli McIntosh

Congratulations on taking the first steps into learning new strategies that are unique and proven to be effective in practice and by research. The strategies are easy to implement because they are founded on equality, positivity and win–win principles. They are equally well accepted by everyone in business from employees to managers and owners. The beauty of the systems is also that they are self-regulating and self-perpetuating, providing staff with strategies to assess and resolve problems for themselves. This is achieved while keeping the business interests in focus and reducing wasted time in managing the people. There are also tools that provide a structure to assess employees' performance and behaviour is at the level expected with built-in legal protection for the business.

Establishing a Positive Culture and standards is the foundation for this process, so that is the starting point. This step alone will provide business owners and managers with a refreshing and liberating approach for resolving the traditionally difficult workplace challenges. The following chapters will progressively work through the other issues with tools and techniques for the Positive resolution of common business challenges, with many of these solutions being new or unique.

Making the decision to move the business to Positive Culture is usually a decision that is made from the top. Although this is usually the case, there have been organisations where it was started by middle-management and the results were so dramatic that senior management could see the benefits and came on board. The benefits are so obvious and the principles so universal that the decision should be easy. However once committed to the process, everyone including and especially managers and owners need to follow the principles themselves and Walk the Talk and lead by example.

The best starting point is to look at the Mission or Vision Statement of the company and review any Culture statements that are in place. It really does not matter whether you call it a Mission, Vision or Aim but there has to be very clearly stated with a clear endpoint or direction for the business so everyone can know what the business is trying to achieve.

The other important aspect of Vision and Mission Statements is that they need to be exciting, motivational and set high. They allow workers to always be aiming to improve performance and be proud of their company's principles. The aim should always to be the best in your field, and to be recognised as the best! Always aim high so that everyone will stretch to improve and people will often achieve more than they ever expected. It is understood that all businesses need to make a profit but it is the higher principles that will motivate the staff and increase your market share when your values resonate with the customers.

The Mission or Vision Statements should be a short statement reflecting what is the organisation is trying to achieve and how that will be done. The document as a whole needs to explain what it stands for, its higher goals, ethics and consideration around sustainability, community, equity, tolerance and non-discrimination.

Hence this is a very important document to spend the time and effort developing a clear direction and culture to ensure the business stays on track in the long term. Once developed and clearly established in writing, these Statements need to be reinforced at every level of the business immediately and over time to ensure dilution does not occur.

Having high-level Vision improves the chance of employees 'buying in' and when they do, they will show loyalty and commitment to the business with more enthusiasm and better productivity. While this is nebulous and hard to measure, these employees go far beyond expectations to help when difficult situations arise and they actively promote the business's reputation and qualities.

From the customer perspective, the vision and mission statements allow the principles of the business to be understood in the community. When quality services and commitment to support the community are both offered, strong connections are made with customers resulting in loyalty and them promoting your business. Word of mouth is a very powerful form of advertising, continues for the long term and is free! This emotional connection and the support rely on the business being true to its vision and performing in the way that has been promised over the long term.

There are many discussions specifying the difference between Mission and Vision. This is the "What" that the business is all about – brief, hard hitting, able to be attached to business cards or logos. The Mission is strictly speaking the "How" that business is going to achieve the vision. It is usually longer and details who does what, to whom and the outcome.

There can be several elements included in the statement – the purpose, the products and services and the values. The definitions actually don't really matter as the key is the message that is being conveyed so that needs to be really clear. An example of this is where Johnson and Johnson have a "Credo" that lays out their Vision, Mission and Culture merged in a one page document.

Examples

Microsoft:
"There will be a computer on every desk and in every home running Microsoft software." (Bill Gates, 1977)

"To empower every person and every organisation on the planet to achieve more." (Satya Nadella, CEO Microsoft 2015)

Sweetgreen Restaurants:
"Sweetgreen is a destination for delicious food that is both healthy for you and aligned with your values. We source local and organic ingredients from farmers we know and partners we trust, supporting our communities and creating meaningful relationships with those around us. We exist to create experiences where passion and purpose come together."

This is strong because of the inclusion of the readers with *your values* and the community responsibility as they *support* the locals and *develop relationships*. They then go on and list their core values of win, win, win; think sustainably; keep it real; add the sweet touch; make an impact. Their passion is evident and their commitments are clear.

Pfizer Pharmaceuticals:
"We dedicate ourselves to humanity's quest for longer, healthier, happier lives through innovation in pharmaceutical, consumer and animal products."

The purpose is therefore the *quest for longer, healthier, happier lives,* with the business being *pharmaceutical, consumer and animal products* and the values being *innovation.*

Mackay GP Superclinic:
"To be recognised as providing the best general practice service in the region. We aim to give each patient, at every attendance a quality service that sets new standards in quality, value, friendliness and professionalism."

This vision goes beyond providing the best service, it also is aiming to be recognised as the best service and leading the industry. The values also reflect the effort for constant quality improvement into the future and that new standards are always being set, aiming to improve standards across the country.

Developing the Vision with Staff

In the process of developing the organisation's vision, it is useful to include the employees as much as possible. While in some organisations this is not practical or relevant, when it is done it produces the immediate staff buy-in. Their involvement also sends a strong message that their views are important and that they add value to the organisation.

Using a facilitator that is experienced in this process can be useful to ensure that everyone gets heard and the outcome is valuable. It also ensures that the process is not highjacked by a verbal minority and that high-level Vision and Mission Statements are achieved. Usually there will be a few alternative choices that are developed and if the best is not clear, the management or owners will need to make the final choice.

Vision and Mission Statements can also be developed using the tools supplied online from our resources area where you can work through the processes with full explanations.

When the Vision and Mission Statements are finalised they should be distributed to all the staff and displayed publicly at all your outlets. This should include your business offices, on all your websites, social internet pages and apps. The target audience is both the staff and customers to spread the understanding of the high ideals and aims of the business.

Creating Positive Culture Statements

After the broad Vision and Mission Statements are in place, the next step is to develop the more detailed standards of behaviour and operation that will allow the vision and mission to be achieved. This is then getting down into the detailed culture and behaviours within the organisation or the 'Culture Statements'.

Culture Statements for service industries are likely to contain more detail around communication and customer service while industrial companies are going to have a higher focus on safety issues, training and compliance. Some industries have specific requirements like confidentiality in medical and legal businesses but there are many shared culture statements that cross all businesses.

Just like the Vision Statement, the Culture Statements should be set high for pride and have excellence as the target. However, the basic areas still need to be covered like honesty, avoiding denigration, gossip and sarcasm and dealing with conflict. While these may seem very obvious to most people, it is very important that they are clearly stated and established as unbreakable principles and so that you can fall back on these if they are ever breached. Other basic culture areas are teamwork, effective communications and the expectation that these standards will always be met.

Quality issues like excellence, consistency, professionalism, integrity and ownership also need to be covered. Industrial companies will include safety and environmental statements and quality improvement of systems.

There are also high-level Culture Statements that can be included to cover areas like life-balance, joy and happiness, gratitude and abundance. As an example, here are the Culture Statements that were established for our large multicentred medical group.

Culture Statements

Excellence – *I always provide work and services to an exceptional quality that adds value to all involved with my work. I constantly strive to improve my own performance and look at ways of continuously improving the systems within the business with innovation.*

Professionalism – *My work, behaviour, speech and demeanour reflect the standard of the business and I therefore always perform all my duties in a professional manner well above the levels expected by clients and peers alike.*

Communication – *I always speak positively of my fellow team members, clients, professionals and the business in both public and private. All my words are for good purpose, using positive and empowering terms. I do not use or listen to gossip, profanity, sarcasm or derogatory language and I will only speak constructively. I greet and farewell people using their names and take responsibility for responses to my communication.*

Consistency – *I provide consistent service levels within my work so clients and team members will feel comfortable dealing with me at all times.*

Confidentiality – *I acknowledge that all information about the clients, practice, business, professionals and all the staff remains strictly confidential to all persons outside the business including my partner and family. I will not even discuss issues already known to external individuals. I may discuss general medical issues or situations that are de-identified and in no way can be connected to the persons involved. I acknowledge that breach of confidentiality is a dismissible offence without warning.*

Integrity – *I always speak the truth and I deliver what I promise. I only make offers that I am prepared to keep and I communicate any breakdowns in commitments at the first opportunity. I resolve any broken commitments immediately.*

Ownership – *I take full responsibility for all of my actions, words, outcomes and all that takes place in my life.*

*Team Work_* – *I focus on working within the team cooperatively to achieve the best results overall. I am flexible to change my work habits, to learn new skills, to ask for help and to help others with compassion* whenever necessary to achieve team goals. I always focus on solving problems and achieve resolutions, not compromises.

Dealing with Conflict – I acknowledge what is being said may be true for the speaker at that moment. I always apologise for any upsets first and then look for a solution to the problem. I only ever discuss concerns in private with the person concerned.

Systems – I acknowledge that most errors in business result from system failure and not person failure. I therefore constantly look for ways to improve all the systems in operation in the workplace.

Joy and Happiness – I will always make every day a pleasure to enjoy and I will spread that joy and happiness to all those around me, making the workplace fun, positive and a great place to be.

Balance – I have a balanced approach to life, remembering that my physical, emotional, spiritual and family life is just as important as my financial achievements. I do not take problems from work home or bring problems from home to work.

Gratitude – I am a truly grateful person. I say thank you and show my appreciation often and in different ways. I celebrate my wins and the wins of the team and patients. I consistently catch myself and others doing things right….

Abundance – I allow abundance in all areas of my life and I deserve abundance due to my positive actions. I respect my self-worth and that of others. I easily give and receive abundance and acknowledge that I receive it back to the level that I give it out. I acknowledge that positive actions result in positive results but the return may not be from the direction expected.

Of particular note is that in the communication statement it is recognised that I *take responsibility for responses to my communication.* So, it is not just enough to say something, it is also your responsibility to ensure that the meaning of what you have said has been correctly understood!

In the Conflict Statement, the staff recognise that the person is stating things that they consider true for them at that time so this reduces the chance of a knee-jerk aggressive reaction.

Within the *Systems* statement, the emphasis is on looking for the systems errors and taking the emphasis off the person involved. Clearly in the more structured industrial areas, this statement may not be true but it is still important to ensure that staff feels safe enough to report errors so that they can be fixed and that the systems can be reviewed.

I take full responsibility for all of my actions, words, outcomes and all that takes place in my life! Notice that this is referring to all of life and not just work. It reinforces the important principle of taking full responsibility for all your actions and outcomes that then gives you the power to change your own future....

The last four culture statements of Joy and Happiness, Balance, Gratitude and Abundance are aimed at the higher levels of personal and spiritual achievement. If your business is able to move your staff to these higher levels of personal functioning, that benefit will flow back to the business with improved inter-personal skills and tolerance for others.

Using the Positive Culture Statements for Quality Control

Using these Culture Statements in businesses is effective to improve attitudes and the atmosphere and will also improve performance. It is important to integrate them into every aspect of the business and they need to be supported and reinforced from the most senior level through every level of the organisation. They also create a powerful tool for management to reduce legal risk and resolve conflict positively when dealing with aggrieved employees.

The positive business approach needs to start at the first interview with prospective employees. The Vision and Culture Statements can be given to the candidate to read and then discuss them. If prodding is needed by then interviewer, you can use questions like "What do you think of these expectations for the workplace?" and "Would you imagine any problems working with these standards for yourself or others in the workplace?"

For the successful candidates, the business Vision and Culture Statement is included in the employment documentation and discussed again with them needing to sign agreeing to comply with the statements, thus legally committing to these standards.

Reinforcement of the Culture Statements should occur in regular staff meetings, going through them to give examples of compliance and any areas that could be improved. Having real life examples to show what to do and what not to do is very effective to create behavioural change. This is because everyone loves stories and the positive and negative outcomes to the different behaviours are usually very obvious.

Another great outcome of such strong culture statements is that if a staff member is out of line in any way, the discussion can be based around the Culture Statements. Nine times out of ten, approaching it in this way results in the employee realising and admitting what they have done wrong themselves and makes the whole process less stressful for everyone. In dealing with this wayward behaviour, the behaviour can be discussed directly and how it does not comply with the culture, or the established culture can be discussed first and ask if they have any problems in this area.

For example:

Manager – "Hello Jane, thanks for coming to see me. How are things going for you?" with general but short discussion to make sure there is no other major crisis going on in their life or in your business.

Manager – "You know we really appreciate your great work on front counter and you are one of the best receptionists we have (or similar positive statement). Today I was wanting to talk about our Communication Culture Statement that talks about 'always speaking positively of my fellow team members, clients... and that all my words are for good purpose.' Do you remember that? How do you feel you have been handling this area?"

The staff member in most cases will immediately talk about the event that you have concerns about and then the Culture Statements can be used to direct the solution. This can be driven by the manager asking questions like "How do you think you could have handled the situation differently?" or "How could you have created a different outcome if you were faced with that situation again?"

If the staff member has no knowledge of the events that you are trying to resolve, then the manager has to bring up that particular event and discuss it themselves. This needs to be approached without prejudgment, no matter how obvious it seems to you from the story that you have heard. Start with questions to get the story correct first, for example:

"There was situation that I heard about where between you and Kate had a heated discussion and you stormed off saying that she was 'a useless so and so'. Can you tell me what happened there please?"

The story from Jane's side will be brought out and you are not prejudging. When you have the story and assess one party (or both) to be at fault, the next step is to say, "So how do think this action fits with our Culture Statement?" and then "How could you have handle the situation differently to get a better outcome?" Mostly the employee tells you what they need to change and as the manager, you can help them refine their improved actions and make sure that they know to use the better course of actions next time. They can also be asked if they see any difficulty in maintaining this appropriate behaviour if similar situations arise in the future.

Preventing the whole situation arising in the first place is possible by creating the Positive Culture and training staff in the standards. This means that as the standards are strengthened in the business, there are less and less of these situations that arise and the managers do not have to keep 'stamping out the fires'.

Many more examples and training modules with these processes and staff management solutions are available in our Positivity Principles Resources area online.

It is always a shame when simple civilised human behaviour needs to be documented as an expected standard. Unfortunately, as we have experienced in our business life, if the specific behaviours are not clearly listed and explained, many people have standards in their own life that do not rise to the professional expectations of successful business. As a result, they think that it is fine to behave in make comments that they consider to be the truth that is hugely damaging or derogatory to individuals or the business.

As these systems get more established, staff members that are not coming up to the standard will often leave the organisation of their own free will and the need for disciplinary action or official dismissal processes is reduced dramatically. When they are needed, they are much easier as employees will usually see for themselves that they are not compliant and the manager will usually have been seen to be actively supporting them. This makes everyone's life better as it is less stressful for the managers and being called into to see the manager is no longer such a dreaded experience.

Everyone needs to remember that both parties want the employee to continue working, the person to earn the money and the business to have the productivity. As a result, they are both there to fix whatever the problem is so they both want the same thing. This understanding changes the dynamic in the meetings with the employee taking the approach of what can they do to perform as required, while the manager's approach is to work out how to change the behaviour so it has the desired performance outcomes. If the antagonistic approach is removed, solutions present themselves.

The fact that the culture statements are clearly and simply stated allows everyone to know how they should behave and equally that all the negative behaviours are unacceptable. The flow on result is that every worker develops the skills to watch their own behaviours and everyone will learn the skill to pleasantly and positively pull their peers into line when necessary.

This is therefore creating a self-regulating system where each employee at every level is working for the positive improvement of the workplace atmosphere. This also means that the team leaders, line managers and higher management will have an easier job to maintain the positive and supportive environment that they are trying to develop.

Summary

Develop a clear Vision and Mission Statement for everyone to understand and follow with detailed Culture Statements about standards of behaviour, operations and interactions within the organisation. This sets high standards and keep those statements at the forefront of every employee's mind from interviews, employment contracts, regular business operations and for staff disciplinary processes.

With every staff member monitoring their own behaviour and others around them, the organisation will become more self-regulating. This reduces the requirement of the team leaders or managers to intervene and when intervention is required, the system in place makes the process easier, non-confrontational and supportive.

CHAPTER 2

Accentuate the Positive, Eliminate the Negative – at Work!

CHAPTER 2

Accentuate the Positive, Eliminate the Negative – at Work!

"As we look forward into the next century, leaders will be those who empower others."

– Bill Gates

Everyone will have experienced or heard about workplace environments that are 'toxic'. It is a well-known phenomenon with profound effects on morale, health and productivity – so everyone loses. Hopefully everyone has also experienced the pleasure of being in a positive and supportive environment and the difference is profound in every way.

In the Positive Workplace staff members are supportive of each other, working together for the good of the clients, company and each other. There is no criticism, sarcasm, gossip, denigration or negative comments. Productivity is better and work feels easier and problems are overcome faster and with everyone pulling together. Job satisfaction, respect and recognition of achievements is all better, sickness and staff turnover is lower. Work just feels like a wonderful place to be and everyone looks forward to turning up every day! Interactions with customers are better, resulting in better services provided, and this leads to better job security and a viable, profitable business. There are also personal health benefits for everyone in this environment. This is clearly a win–win–win situation in every direction.

So is this utopia actually possible? Is this utopia worth working towards? If you work in a full-time job, you will be spending more of your waking hours in your workplace than any other single environment. Therefore, it is really important that this part of your life is pleasurable, joyful and that it boosts your energy and vitality.

The fact is that the atmosphere in every workplace is determined purely by the attitudes and behaviours of the workers in that space. Therefore, as one of the workers, the atmosphere in your workplace is completely within your control and your work colleagues!

Obviously to create a wonderful, happy, positive work environment, it requires widespread cooperation to create this new way of interacting. The first step in this process is to recognise and remove negativity – in a nice way. Everyone needs to learn the techniques to resolve interpersonal conflict with positivity and eliminate personal attacks and denigration. We will teach you the new techniques of Positive Mindfulness Cognition™ in this book and these will help in every area of your life. Positive Mindfulness Cognition™ (PMC) is having mindful awareness and taking positive control over your thoughts.

For the culture of positivity to be created, support is needed from the top. Business owners and managers need to "walk the talk" and lead by example. This movement of positivity has been achieved within organisations from the middle levels as well with buy in from the senior executives when the benefits were so obvious that they had to change their behaviours! As the benefits to business are obvious, recognisable and easy to adopt so it is a relatively easy concept to "sell" to senior management. Even more wonderful is the cost and risk is low and the potential benefits are immense!

It is interesting when organisations that adopt Positivity as their expected culture, the whole group develops much more interpersonal respect, appreciation and empathy. The results are tangible, so let's get started with each one of you individually and look at cleaning up any negativity from your own thoughts and then look at how we can spread the positivity to everyone else.

Being Mindful of your Thoughts – Listen to your Inner Voice

The technique you will learn here to recognise and eliminate your negative thoughts is unique, effective and proven by research. Once you have the skills, you can teach your partner, children, friends and social groups and you will start creating better environments in every area of your life. But let's start with you and the workplace.

Everyone's mind generates thoughts continuously. This is commonly known as your inner voice, internal dialogue or 'mind chatter'. It is like having a conversation with yourself, even though most people would not admit that they "talk to themselves". We establish the tone and nature of our internal dialogue from a very young age, and as we grow older, this dialogue changes according to our life experiences.

This dialogue does have a huge bearing on how you feel, what you expect for yourself and influences every decision you make. The majority of people believe the messages from this inner voice and do not question these thoughts at all. This mind chatter is often negative and self-destructive, creating self-sabotage that undermines success often because the person thinks they don't deserve it or will fail. This inner voice is so powerful that even when you consciously want an outcome very strongly, if you don't believe you deserve it, your actions will sabotage yourself and cause you to fail.

For example, having internal thoughts of "This project at work will never be completed on time" directly blocks the creative mind's normal process of looking for solutions to manage the problem. As a result, the effort put into the project is reduced and creative solutions are not searched for and the project fails. The mindset and subconscious thoughts are therefore a very powerful self-fulfilling prophesy – if you think you will fail, you are right. Equally though if you think you will succeed, you will also be right!

The mind chatter affects you (the reader) in every aspect of life – how well you learn, what you are good at, whether you are good with the opposite sex, how good you are as a parent, friend, boss, worker etc. Your mind chatter or internal dialogue is something that has been cultivated over your entire life, influenced by your most respected teachers and reinforced by repeated events over the years. It is therefore well-entrenched and deep-seated, with its roots in events and statements that you are probably not even aware of.

So our first piece of advice is that changing these long-established habits will not occur overnight and will take some persistence and effort – but it CAN BE DONE!

Mind chatter will therefore be going on inside all of us and be with most of us all the time. The big question is: what is your internal voice telling you?

It may be telling you positive and supporting statements like –

"Yes, you can achieve this goal."
"Yes, you are a great worker/beautiful/valuable asset to the company"
"You deserve to get this job/partner/income."
"You have a wonderful life and will succeed."

Or it may be making negative and self-destructive statements like –
"You always fail."
"You never get the gorgeous girlfriend/boyfriend."
"They will never give you a raise."
"You don't deserve the good things in life."

Start listening to your own thoughts and see if they are positive and encouraging or negative and discouraging. Practice watching these thoughts so you can see, hear of feel them whenever they come to the surface. This is important because recognising them is the first step to their elimination.

As Lao Tzu states, "thoughts become words" and negative thoughts become negative words that have a negative impact on everyone around you. Hence the key is to stop the negative thought as it is formed and not let it become words, action, habits, character and your destiny! Positive thoughts lead to positive actions and a better outcome.

Many people believe that the thoughts inside their heads are beyond their control. This is absolutely not the case and it is just a learned habit – therefore a new habit can be learnt in its place. Also we will teach you a simple 3-step process that rapidly flips those negative thoughts into positive ones. This is the basis of Positive Mindfulness Cognition™ where you become mindful of your thoughts and actively control what you think.

We have coined the term "Negative Impulsive Thoughts" or NITs because the negative thoughts are occurring impulsively and the similarities to nits which is a common term for head lice are remarkable. They are both highly contagious, spread rapidly from person to person, are difficult to recognise and need repeated treatments to eliminate them. Negative thoughts are like an unrecognised epidemic that is affecting almost every one of us and can affect every area of our lives with devastating effects. They lead to unhappiness, self-doubt and lack of success.

In the workplace, they produce destruction of self-esteem and self-worth, job satisfaction, productivity and profitability. Negative thoughts need to recognised and eliminated, so let's move onto the Magic Questions to recognise Negativity and the 3-step process to flip them into positives.

The Magic Questions to Recognise Negative Thoughts

To make the process of NIT recognition quick, easy and instantly effective, we have created three simple questions that will allow you to identify them. This allows everyone to rapidly and easily assess any thoughts, words or actions from within yourself or from external sources. These need to be memorised to be brought out in rapid-fire for any situation to immediately recognise the Negativity so you can then get into the treatment process and eliminate them.

The Magic Questions to identify NITs are:

1. Is this information the truth and *confirmed* to be the truth?

2. Does this cause any negative impact on myself or anyone else?

This will give you to the clear decision as to whether the information is worth bringing into your life and propagating or whether you need to eliminate the NIT. To expand on each question, think about the following information for each:

Question 1: Is the information based on the truth and confirmed as such?
Is there any doubt as to the source?
Has the information been received from both sides of the situation?

Question 2: Is it constructive or is it destructive to myself or others?
Is it helpful or unhelpful to myself and others?
Will it make me and the people around me feel good or bad?
Will it boost us up or will it cut us down?
Is this thought going to help everyone move closer towards their goals, or is it limiting or blocking anyone in any way?
Is it helping everyone move forward, or is it slowing someone down?

For Question 1, not only does the information need to be true, but it also needs to be confirmed to be true. When faced with statements where the truth is not yet confirmed, keep that information on hold for later consideration until the truth is revealed. Sometimes it is important to ask the person directly or get more specific information about the statements, like who exactly said that or believes that to be the case. What are the words that the person actually used? Get the full details of the information, preferably from the person who is meant to have said it before you jump to conclusions.

From Question 2, you will be categorising them into constructive or destructive thoughts and this will give you another key as to whether the items are NITs or not. It will give you clues as to whether you should act on this thought, let the thought turn into words and actions or dismiss the thought.

This question also helps recognise information that may be the truth but is going to be detrimental or unhelpful for yourself or others. There are many truths that will clearly have a negative impact. They may appear to be constructive by being camouflaged with a veneer of a compliment. However, on closer inspection, they are NITs in disguise.

Common examples of NITs in the workplace

"God, I hate this job."
"I just can't wait for the end of the day."
"We'll never be able to complete this contract on time."
"The boss is only interested in money."
"She is so manipulative/trashy/up herself/pompous/nasty, etc."
"He/she is useless and doesn't pull his/her weight."
"Have you heard that he/she is having an affair with…?"
"I heard he/she was fired from her last job because…"

Quick Guide to Other Negative Terms

Gossip, sarcasm and innuendo:

These are all not based on the truth so they will definitely fail the first question as well as failing both question 2 and 3. These usually have an underlying vindicate cause so should be eliminated from the workplace as a cultural expectation.

Malicious NITs:

NITs may also be used deliberately and maliciously by someone for their own benefit in some way while being detrimental to yourself or others. These divide and upset the staff and the malicious person will often tell the different people different versions to set the two parties against each other.

It is certainly very important that when you come across a NIT, you do not allow it to propagate further by spreading it to others. One option here is to acknowledge the potential of the facts being wrong with a comment like "I am not sure if it is true, so let's wait until we get confirmation of that before we jump to conclusions." Another option is to say "That certainly doesn't sound like the Jo that I know. I think we should wait and see if that is the truth before jumping to conclusions."

Using "Always, Never, Everyone, No one":

This is another breed of Negativity as the propagator is trying to prove they are correct with the all-encompassing terms. By definition, this actually makes them false as very few things are ever that comprehensive. So anytime you hear someone using the terms "always, never, everyone and no one" with negative intent, it will usually mean that you are dealing with a NIT!

We encourage you to ask a few more questions, even if it is only in your head, as you will be finding NITs galore in the "always, never, everyone, no one" statements.

These terms are fine with positive intent – for example "I will always strive for the best" or "My intentions are always honourable".

3-Step Process for Treating Negative Thoughts

The treatment of Negative thoughts needs to be fast and immediate and the Positive Mindfulness Cognition™ technique is easy, practical and very effective. It is effective when used in workplaces, personal lives, families, relationships, sports and medicine. It has also been used in a wide variety of industries and in different cultures and works very well without boundaries.

This process will need to be practiced repeatedly so that it can become a habit, occur automatically and eventually occur subconsciously in your mind.

The 3-step process for Negative Thoughts is the STOP, DROP and ROLL technique:

1. STOP – freeze it, net it, hold it still while you assess it
2. DROP – destroy the negative thought
3. ROLL – replace it with a positive alternative

The most effective way of performing these three steps will depend on how you personally process information. There are three ways that people process information and these are visual, auditory and kinaesthetic – in other words seeing, hearing or feeling. Whichever of these areas you naturally and easily use will be the most effective process for you to use for any learning process and also to break the NIT habit. If you are a visual person you will be able to use your visual processes to destroy the NITs, if you are auditory you will do best with sound strategies and kinaesthetic you will be best to use emotional strategies.

People commonly have a blend of these types, so you may able to relate to more than one category. However, understanding how you and your staff learn best will help in selecting the best strategies in dealing with NITs and in teaching your staff new processes. It is also a very important skill when dealing with others because using the correct communication process will have dramatic effects on getting your message across.

Here is a guide to show you the sorts of comments the different processing types will use.

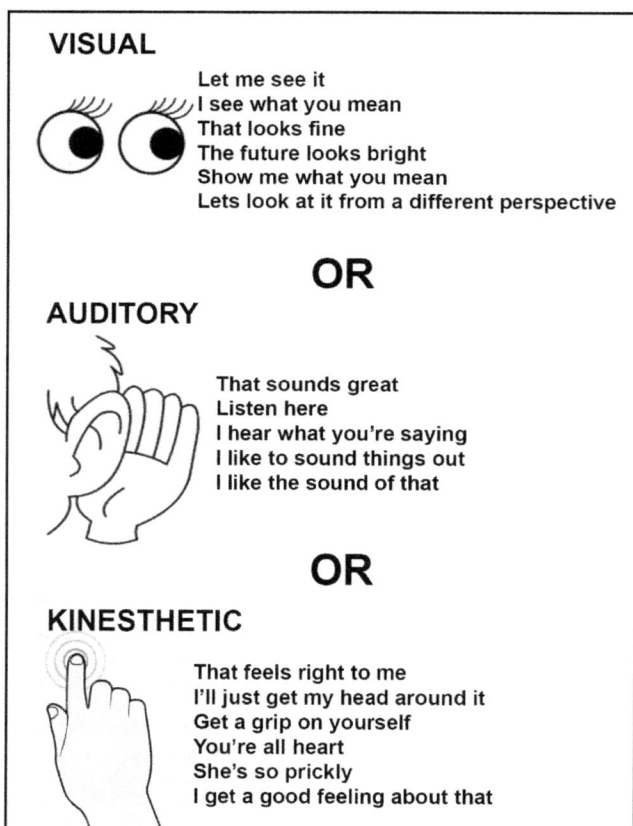

VISUAL

Let me see it
I see what you mean
That looks fine
The future looks bright
Show me what you mean
Lets look at it from a different perspective

OR

AUDITORY

That sounds great
Listen here
I hear what you're saying
I like to sound things out
I like the sound of that

OR

KINESTHETIC

That feels right to me
I'll just get my head around it
Get a grip on yourself
You're all heart
She's so prickly
I get a good feeling about that

Diagram 1. Visual, Auditory and Kinaesthetic processing

STOP. First you need to stop or hold the thought. If you are visual, you would see the words and could stop them by freezing the letters, netting them or just stop them as if on a computer. The auditory people could think of it like a recording that you pause or stop the tape recording with a screech. For the kinaesthetic person, will need to cut all emotional reactions to it, localise the feeling and move that feeling outside of your body and hold it there.

Your aim is to stop and hold the thought so it can't escape. This will give you the time to assess it and destroy it if necessary.

DROP. This second step is the removal process. For the visual operators, you can imagine PacMan munching the words, blast them with a bazooka, press the delete button or destroy them with a flame thrower – whatever works for you! The auditory processors would best imagine that you hear the words being rewound backwards and deleted with the high-pitched squealing that you get – Woolloomooloo! The kinaesthetic processors need to detach yourselves from the feeling and get away from it by throwing it away, freezing, blasting, burning or deleting it.

ROLL. This is the process of rolling the Negative Thought into a Positive alternative. For example, if the thought was "I am stupid and I will never get this right", you need to immediately replace it with a statement like "I am a good learner and every new skill takes practice. Mistakes are part of the learning process so I am getting better with every attempt".

This replacement of the Negative Thought with a Positive one needs to be done within seconds, and is a skill that improves with practice. Delay at this point gives the NIT the chance to recover and regain strength. Like any bad habit, you can't leave a vacant space; you have to put a new

---

habit in its place. By practicing the process, you will respond faster and it will become more automatic over time.

Here are some examples of the Positive alternative to common NITs.

Table 2. Changing NITs into PATS

NITs	PATs
1. I can't do it	Says who? Of course, I can do it. I'll keep practising until I get it right.
2. That's impossible	Of course, it can be done. Other people have done greater things, so I just need to work out the solution and harness my own imagination.
3. I am stupid	Everyone makes mistakes, and each time I attempt it, I get better and better.
4. He is better than I am	He is really good at that skill so I should learn from him to improve my skills in that area. We all have different areas of expertise.
5. Nobody likes me	Of course, some people like me, and with my wonderful positive thinking I will be a joy to be around.
6. We will never be able to finish this project	This is a very challenging project so we will need to work very hard and cooperatively together and create solutions to each barrier that arises.
7. Nothing ever works out for me	This has not worked this time. What can I learn from it to have a better chance of success next time? I will get better with every attempt.
7. I always have bad luck	I make my own luck, and with a positive attitude, I will attract luck as positive thoughts attract positive outcomes.

8. Everyone is talking about me	I need to keep remembering that people usually act like this out of jealousy. What people want to talk about is up to them, but at least I know that I am doing the right thing, can hold my head up high. Their rumours/criticisms/comments will be shown for what they are at some time.
9. This business is only interested in profits	We need to focus on quality service and efficiency as the viability of the business is purely dependant on being profitable. The more successful we are, the more our jobs are guaranteed.
10. It's so busy, I haven't had time for a lunch break	Isn't it great that it is so busy that I haven't had time for a lunch break! The business is doing really well and my job will be secure. Or How great will that be for my figure!
11. Why is it that I am always the one doing the extra work?	Isn't it great that I am performing so well that I am able to carry the other staff. My job will be secure and it is likely to get me promotions in the future. Keep up the great work!

Positivity and 'No NITs' Training

Positivity, like cleanliness and motivation, requires regular reinforcement to maintain the high standards that are desired. It is not going to occur if it is done once and then ignored for months and even if you have created a positive environment successfully, you need to constantly reinforce and cultivate that position. If at any stage you start getting doubts about whether it is worth it (a classic Negative Thought) you only need to consider the consequences of a toxic environment filled workplace with sarcasm, denigration and back-stabbing compared to the utopia we are striving towards.

Positive Mindfulness Cognition™ training can be effectively performed by direct staff training in 1–2 hours, covering the recognition and elimination of negative thoughts. This allows a lively discussion around the different negative thoughts that everyone has so they all know that they are "normal". More importantly when individuals discuss the effects negative comments have, the huge impact on emotional state or productivity is better understood by everyone.

Clearly, the PMC training reinforces the Culture Statements very well, so they should be reinforced during these sessions. Additionally, this positive approach to life that is learned at work will benefit all the staff members in their personal lives as well. Explaining this to the staff creates the expectation of improvements in their relationships and their performance at home – and it does work.

This training will need to be repeated within the workplace on a regular basis with the frequency dependent on the needs of the business. The repeated training is important to reinforce and establish these standards as the status quo. It is interesting that even when the same training programs are repeated, staff will usually be happy to attend as they get new benefits every time and the sessions are enjoyable and motivational. There are always improvements in attitude, motivation and improved interpersonal relationships.

Training can be provided by motivated in house staff or external trainers depending on the business needs. The most important aspect is that the trainers are skilled, knowledgeable and believe in the process as this is fundamental for the staff to buy in. There are also video modules in the resources section of this book or the websites that can be accessed, including free modules.

Positive Mindfulness Cognition™ training has been used in several different industry groups and research has confirmed significant business and staff outcomes. This confirms our personal business experience of the effectiveness of the training. The research shows that atmosphere and workplace satisfaction levels have increased with a single two-hour "Positive Culture" training modules. There was a 15% improvement in optimism scores and a 20% improvement is resilience to negative events after a single Positivity Training session. Workplace atmosphere and staff satisfaction levels at work were dramatically improved.

Exposing NITs in the Workplace

Once the 'No NITs' training has occurred and the staff is aware of negative thoughts and words, individuals can be pulled up when they let NITs escape. However the way this is done is very important because it needs to be performed in a positive way or the outcome would be opposite to the desired positive one we are targeting. Therefore, all comments should be Positive without personal criticism, derision or denigration.

So keep it all light-hearted and fun. It should not be critical or nasty as we know that everyone has negative thoughts that need to be controlled and everyone needs practice. Make sure you are being positive and supportive and if they can't think of a positive alternative, make a suggestion for them.

Some workplaces have developed a specific process like blowing a raspberry, calling out 'NIT alert!' or having a jar where every NIT results in a small fine and the staff enjoy a night out or positive event with the proceeds. Or the presence of the Negative comment could be highlighted with a simple "That sounds like a NIT – perhaps you can flip it into a better alternative?"

Here are some other examples of being Positive when dealing with Negatives:

"I used to have thoughts like that but I found better results by approaching it in this way."

"You are such a kind person, I am sure you would be horrified if you hurt someone which happened with a comment like that. Perhaps if you made that comment this way, the situation would not have arisen."

"I am sure you did not mean to upset Tina in that situation. A different way of approaching the situation that may work better for everyone would be to..."

If you are faced with a pessimistic comment like "What's the point? We always fail!" – you could respond with "Do we always fail? I don't think so. There are many wonderful successes that we have had in the past that prove we can be successful and we are a great team that is excellent at overcoming challenges. These recent struggles just mean that the success will be even sweeter. We need to keep on getting better and better with each attempt."

"Everyone agrees that this is a stupid way of working." The response could be to ask the person "Who amongst the staff agree with that? If so, is there better alternative?" Is it really everyone, or is it just one person with a big mouth that wants to say it's 'everyone' to back themselves up?

At the end of the day, it is owner or manager's decision that decides how the systems should work and if that is you, it is you that will pay the price with losses if you are wrong. The group of 'everyone' is not paying the bills – so you as the manager or owner, makes the decision, get the staff on board with positive explanations and watch how it goes. If you were wrong and it fails, you learn the lesson, you pay the price and you can do it differently the next time!

The bottom line is that negative thoughts or words should never be allowed to escape in workplace unchallenged and always need to be recognised, eliminate and replaced with positive alternatives.

Ensure that all your thoughts, words and actions at work (and in your life) are based on positivity. You will find the outcomes are dramatically better with the ripple effect of positivity spreading outwards to motivate and inspire everyone for better effort and more creative solutions.

As the culture of positivity becomes more established, the pleasure for everyone being at work becomes stronger and even customers entering the workplace can 'feel' the difference. Everyone wins!

Summary

Start paying attention to your inner voice and use the Magic Questions to detect Negative Thoughts. The three-step technique of Stop, Drop and Roll can then be used to eliminate them. Use the best method for you whether it is visual, auditory or kinaesthetic to stop that Negativity in its tracks, destroying it and then rolling it over into a Positive Affirmative Thought or PAT.

Create a work environment of Positivity by recognising and eliminating negative thinking and using positive processes in all your thoughts, words and deeds. Yes, you can control your own thoughts and create a wonderful, Positive workplace environment!

CHAPTER 3

Five Steps to Positively Manage Mistakes

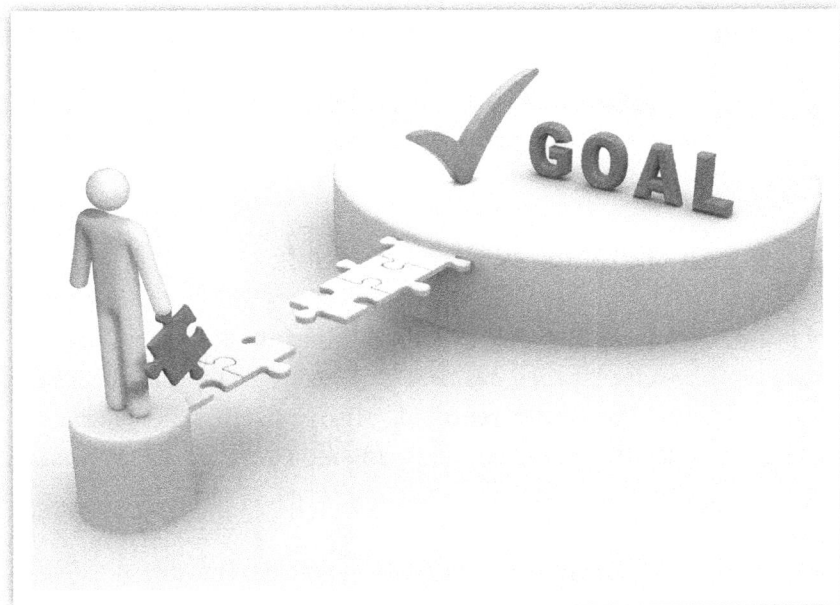

CHAPTER 3

Five Steps to Positively Manage Mistakes

"Mistakes are just stepping stones to success."

– Unknown

Every successful person and every successful business has created that success by a series of actions, many of which have failed, been reviewed and then improved. By constantly repeating this process, success is eventually achieved. Failures and mistakes are essential stepping-stones to high levels of success in any field as the processes are practiced and refined. This then brings us to the first step in Positively Managing Mistakes:

Step ① Use Mistakes as Learning Tools

Every business and every worker in every business will make mistakes at some point. A well-managed business will ensure that these mistakes are not dangerous, costly or repeated. Also, mistakes need to be considered to be learning experiences for the individual or the business so that performance can be progressively improved.

If the culture of business always handles mistakes with this positive approach, they are not hidden under the carpet and can be dealt with openly and rapidly. Further steps can then immediately be put into action to fix the problem and avoid delays. This then prevents the damaging ripple effect from spreading outwards and avoids escalating problems in the business, customer service and staff problems.

This culture needs to be set by the owners or managers within the business to allow the workers to be confident that they are in a safe environment for mistakes to be acknowledged. Only if that is the case will mistakes be immediately reported and resolved.

Step ❷ Take 100% Responsibility and Apologise Immediately

As soon as a mistake is recognised as having occurred, the offended party needs to receive an apology. If this is in a customer service industry and it is a client or customer that has suffered as a result of the error, they need to be approached and informed of the problem with an immediate apology. If the mistake is within the business, the staff member affected or the supervisor running that system needs to be informed and receive the apology.

For this to occur, one of the key success principles needs to be in place and this is that everyone in the business should take 100% responsibility for everything that they say and do, and the results of their actions.

This principle is well described in many success books from Napoleon Hill's book *Think and Grow Rich*, published in 1937, to more recent books by Jack Canfield such as *The Success Principles* and our previous book *Mastering Negative Impulsive Thoughts*. It is not a new principle; it has stood the test of time and continues to be the cornerstone to taking control of your own life and determining your future success and happiness. It is equally important in business.

Learning to take 100% responsibility about everything in your life is very empowering and results in you being 100% in control of your future. If you are not able to take full responsibility, then you will never be able to fully control your life. The great news is that by taking responsibility for where you are right now, it gives you the power to get to where you want to be in the future!

Within the workplace, everyone needs to take 100% responsibility for their actions and the results of those actions. By taking 100% responsibility for the situation, the worker acknowledges their full responsibility for the situation directly to the offended party. Any anger by the offended party is then usually limited towards that one person and does not spread to involve any further staff.

A typical example is when a receptionist forgets to put a client's file up for an appointment, so the professional is not aware that they are waiting. Time passes and the person in not seen in a timely manner. By immediately taking responsibility and apologising to the client, the receptionist prevents the mistake being blamed on the other staff, the professional or the business more generally. Equally, if it is the professional that is running behind, it should be them that immediately apologises and explains the reason for the delay.

The 'ripple effect' is the term we use for the effect of damage spreading outwards to affect everyone around when responsibility is not taken. Without an apology, the angry client is unsettled in the reception area, has a heated discussion at the front desk that upsets the other clients and the other receptionists. They then go in and have an unpleasant consultation and their bad attitude flows them as they go out to pay the bill, spreading the bad feeling to everyone in earshot! All should be stopped at the very beginning with a simple and honest apology at the time of the first mistake!

The other positive result of this action is that the offended customer will, in the majority of cases, accept the sincere apology and reassures the worker that it is 'no problem. The ripple effect is blocked at its source by this immediate action (in most instances).

There are some fundamental principles here that need to be followed. The first is that the apology needs to be sincere – the worker and the business needs to have quality service provision as it's driving philosophy and clearly because that has been breached the person and the business take it seriously, and want to fix it so that it does not ever happen again.

Customers will see and understand if you are serious about quality and service and if you are sincere. If you have any difficulty in being sincere with a customer when something has gone wrong, you need to put yourself in the customers place and consider how it feels for them.

Forget all the difficulties about your own situation, how much work is on at the moment, how you are short-staffed because of holidays or sickness and everything relating to you. If you were the customer, how would it feel to have had the event happen to you, what are they saying to you about how it is affecting them, and then acknowledge them so that they know that they have been understood. This is a very effective strategy to defuse the situation – you understand how they have suffered, you are sincerely sorry, things will be put in place to make sure that this does not happen again and the problem will be fixed for that person in the best way that can be achieved.

There will be situations where the 'mistake' or event was not personally your fault or that of the business but you may be in front of the person with the problem, receiving the torrents of irritation and negativity. Even in this situation, the solution is to apologise to the person for the mistake with words like "I am very sorry that this has happened to you, Mr Bloggs. I understand it is frustrating that you have come all the way into town to collect the goods and they are not here yet. Obviously we have not received the goods from the XYZ company as they promised to us so we can't give them to you today. What I will do to fix this problem is…"

Even if the error was caused by another staff member in the business or another business, apologise on their behalf if you are dealing with the customer at the time. For example, "I am so sorry that your appointment has been delayed. We made an error here at the front desk and forgot to put your files up for the doctor and it is our fault. I will make sure that the staff are more aware of this so it does not happen again and will get you in to see the doctor immediately".

This then flows nicely into the next step…

Step ❸ Fix the Mistake Fast

Solutions need to be formulated immediately to fix the problem. Take action immediately to remedy the error and the consequent problems that may be a risk. How the errors are handled will depend on the severity of the mistake and its consequences, and when the mistakes are more serious in nature, the response needs to be passed to higher levels of management.

Clearly for minor matters, the person that is in front of the aggrieved customer or dealing with the business situation can deal with immediately. If the solution is not immediately apparent or the matters are more serious in nature, then make the sincere apology to the customer with the comment that the matter will be handed over to the supervisor, manager or owner "to make sure that this is dealt with properly" or "to see how this can be fixed for you".

Another key point is to always stick to the truth. Never say anything that is not 100% true – you are better to say nothing than to "bend" the facts. One strategy here is to say "I am really sorry but I really don't know all the information about this so please let me look into it and I will get back to you. It is a very serious matter and I want to give it my full attention so do not want to give you answers that may not be 100% correct".

Also, everyone does need to keep their 'diplomacy filter' turned on. Consider if there are facts that are better not to be disclosed to the customer because they would reflect badly on the business, on the worker or even on the customer. Filter out information that will not help the situation and only mention other facts and get the problem sorted.

The business owner or manager will need to decide if the event requires compensation of some kind and goodwill is generated much more freely if this compensation is given before the client asks for it. Complementary buffet breakfast at a hotel, a room upgrade, a free facial, an extra half hour on the end of a massage or other relatively low-cost items can be given as compensation. Each business can consider what items they can give away that are relatively low-cost to them but higher value to the client. Having a plan in advance as to what these items are, allows the compensation to be offered early and achieve faster resolution.

From a legal perspective, offers of compensation do not prevent subsequent litigation but approaching the business mistakes with this approach results in much lower risk of claims even from those parties that had justifiable cause. Aggrieved individuals take legal action usually because the company has not taken responsibility of the error, not taken it seriously enough and not recognised the damage caused.

As a result, these strategies significantly protect the business from litigation. I know this because I have used them in my role as Chairman of a community after-hours medical service in a private emergency department. I had to deal with clients for over 20 years with all the complaints and mistakes arising from this high-risk, very complicated medical situations with high emotions and stress. Quality of service was always paramount to our service and there were times when the outcomes or actions were not ideal. Despite such a high-risk situation, all complaints and errors over the 20-year period were dealt with successfully, without a single litigation claim using these strategies. I can therefore confidently say that the strategies work!

Step ④ Focus on the Problem, not the Person

The key factor when dealing with mistakes is to look for the reason the situation arose rather than just attacking the individual who made the 'mistake'. Studies have shown that mistakes in the corporate and business world occur about 80% of the time due to system errors and only 20% of the time due to human errors. Investigations of mistakes will find system errors in four out of five situations and only individual errors one in five.

If everyone in the workforce understands this statistic, the focus can be moved to looking for the system errors rather than making a personal attack. With this understanding the staff will be much more open to report issues and look at ways of improving the systems.

When a mistake occurs, all focus needs to be clearly on the actual problem and why it has occurred. Use phrases like "What is the underlying problem that led to this situation?" or "What is the real problem here that has led to this situation?"

What are the systems in place related to the problem – have the staff had enough training, are the staff members in that role getting the information they need to complete the task, is there a better way to perform the task, is it actually possible to perform the task as expected? If the task is performed adequately by others in the same situation, the individual's performance needs to be assessed. Have they performed better before or have they never been able to do this task? Have they been promoted beyond their level of competence?

The key is to focus on finding the real problem that caused the mistake to occur and avoid automatically blaming the person who made the mistake. Positive outcomes are more likely as this non-confrontational approach avoids conflict and blame-shifting. It also gives individuals the confidence to acknowledge their error and fix it as personal attacks are avoided.

Management do have to step in if an individual repeatedly makes the same mistakes and does not learn from their past actions. Our experience over 30 years in business is that employees who are not performing adequately will leave of their own accord using these Culture Statements and standards. This means that we do not have to step in with the stressful and high-risk dismissal processes that can be challenged legally. This occurs because of the open nature of discussion, ensuring that they take 100% responsibility for their actions and see that they are not suitable to perform the job themselves. This saves lots of work, time, energy, stress as well as business and legal risk!

Commonly problems arise when a key staff member (Jane) is asked to perform certain tasks like collecting data, researching information, however instead of performing the task themselves, it is delegated to a less experienced staff member (Tammy) who runs into problems obtaining the information. Jane has now relinquished all responsibility and presumes Tammy will complete the task and deliver to her the results. In the meantime, Jane forgets about it and at the next meeting is asked to produce the result, responding by blaming Tammy for not following this up.

Staff need to understand that even though they may delegate to another, it is still their responsibility to follow up with the other person to ensure the task is completed. It remains 100% her responsibility and delegation of a task does not transfer responsibility or blame. Alternatively, do the job yourself!

100% responsibility means seeing tasks through till the end and ensuring the final outcome occurs.

Step ⑤ Fix the Underlying Cause

When looking into the cause of mistakes, never prejudge! Make sure that you ask questions that are open, and information gather from both sides of the situation. Do not go into the assessment with only one side of the story or with some prejudged opinion, because it is often wrong! This non-judgmental approach makes the individuals not feel that they are being personally attacked and as a non-judgmental person without taking sides the manager can support the staff member in finding a solution. As a result, a positive solution is much more likely to be found without burning bridges or creating conflict.

The types of questions that the manager or supervisor should be asking are not only about what actually happened, but also why were things done in the way that they were done. What is the reason that you did things in that way? Is that the usual way that this process is performed? Have you been shown any other ways of doing this task? Have you seen other people doing this task like that?

Many problems from customers and within staff arise from communication issues and interpersonal conflict will be addressed in a later chapter. However in the process of assessing mistakes where communication is involved, you will need to ask questions to determine what words were actually said, what was the tone of the voice, what was the 'feeling' that was experienced in that situation and what was that person's understanding of what was happening.

This is important as staff may deny that they have said anything inappropriate or offensive but if that is how it was taken or that was how the recipient 'felt' after the communication, the impact cannot be denied. Obviously, it is the results of the communication that are important and the Culture Statements make everyone responsible for responses to their communication. Therefore even if other 'felt' a certain way about the communication, that staff member should consider how their communication processes can be improved .

Once the information from all sides of any mistake has been obtained, and the underlying reasons for the situation will hopefully be apparent so strategies can be put into place to prevent recurrence of the problem in the future.

By remembering that all mistakes are learning experiences, some reflective questioning to the involved parties should occur after the event and some month later. Questions should be asked like –

What have you learnt from this situation?
What will you do differently next time?
Are you happy that you understand the processes now?
How can we make sure that everyone benefits from this information?

Questions are a Manager's Best Tool

Questions allow managers to understand the what, how and why things happened. They also allow great insights into how individuals are functioning and why they do act in certain ways. They allow you to accurately gauge what they know and what areas of training or skill deficiency they have. So rather than going into situations and telling staff what to do and how to do things, ask questions. If the staff are off-track, leading questions can be used to guide them to create the correct solutions themselves, and they then think it was their idea! Also, because it was them that created the solution, they have ownership so will persist with that new action.

The traditional method of just telling people what to do, gives you no insight into the magnitude or the real nature of the problems that underpin the original mistake.

Summary

Mistakes need to be used as excellent learning experiences in the path to business success. The 5 Steps to Positively Managing Mistakes are:

1. Establish a culture in which mistakes are a tool for learning

2. Take 100% responsibility by the person making the mistake and apologise immediately to the offended party

3. Fix the mistake fast

4. Focus on the problem, not the person that made the mistake

5. Fix and underlying causes of the mistake

CHAPTER 4

Positively Resolving Complaints, Conflict and Aggression

CHAPTER 4

Positively Resolving Complaints, Conflict and Aggression

"The only place for drama is on the stage."

– Eli McIntosh

There are situations in all businesses which occur that create complaints, conflict and aggression, and having all staff skilled to deal with these effectively results in a much happier and productive workplace. It also leads to the workplace being a 'safe' environment where employees are happy to be, resulting in reduced staff turnover.

Complaints, conflict and aggression can occur from within the business employees or from clients. Clearly the management of the two are different but they required the same strategies so they will be discussed here together.

Handling all of these situations in a positive manner requires the staff to have the skills to recognise the signs of an escalating situation, be able to defuse it and communicate effectively and civilly at all times. Preventing these situations arising between staff members requires the Culture Statements to be in place and fully understood by everyone. They establish the behavioural and communication standards required, and if employees are out of line, they can be used to fix the problem.

If the problem arises from people outside the business, then use the following strategies.

The same 5 step plan can be used as explained in the Managing Mistakes chapter:

1. Use the situation as a learning tool
2. Take 100% responsibility and apologise early
3. Fix the problem fast
4. Focus on the problem, not the person
5. Fix any underlying problem

Let's start with a great strategy to prevent escalation of situations.

Don't React. Respond

It is important not to get emotionally involved when faced with conflict or criticism from others – staff or customers. Reactions arise from an emotional base while responding comes from a values base.

Reactions often occur automatically and may be your established habit. Unfortunately, an emotional reaction usually results in an avalanche of escalating drama, confrontation and aggravation. This often turns into personal attacks between the two parties and the real issue is forgotten and quality standards getting lost.

Responding comes from a values base with consideration of the best solution and consideration of the most effective process to achieve that solution. By using high values as the base of your response, you will remain a 'class act' and maintain your dignity and the professional name of the company. So don't react, respond.

When someone is being derogatory or aggressively attacking any of us, the natural reaction is fight or flight – fight back or run away. Neither of these natural reactions will help, so separating yourself from your own negative emotions is important. There is often personal criticism making you feel anger, frustration, disbelief, hurt or disappointment when dealing with the problem. A useful tool to create this separation is to create an imaginary glass bubble around you and use this as a filter to choose what you allow in and what you keep out.

Another tool is the 'box technique' in which you see yourself taking those comments or feelings of hurt and upset, and imagine putting them in a box, wrapping it up and sealing it with rope, tape or ribbon. This Negativity does not serve you in any way so avoid letting it in. The situation needs to be without any personal emotional overlay, as it will impair your judgment.

The other natural and unhelpful reaction is to feel compelled to answer immediately, because we want our side of the story to be heard. Avoid this temptation and use the strategy of saying "That is *very interesting* that you see it that way. Tell me more about what the problem is please". Be empathetic to the other person and ask them to fully explain their point of view. Stay visibly calm, no matter what is happening and as the person gets heard and vents, their anger usually fades.

Using the term 'very interesting' is non-judgmental and puts the complexity of the situation at the forefront, so that the comment is being focused on, and not the person that made the comment. Clearly if you are dealing with a customer, the approach would be more diplomat like "I am really sorry that you are so upset/angry/frustrated. Please leave it with me so that I can work out how to deal with it or discuss it with my seniors".

There are no rules requiring you to react immediately. Counting to ten or walking away gives you time to control your emotions and decide on the best response. Even if you need to physically bite your tongue while counting to ten, do it to prevent the emotional and disruptive reaction while you let the emotional intensity fade. When the emotion has dissipated, you can then consider the actual problem, look for solutions and come back to the person when you are calm. In this way, you maintain your integrity, your class-act status is preserved, and you have avoided a conflict that would have escalated the problem.

Internal Staff Conflict

Well-trained, quality staff will have the skills to resolve internal issues between themselves without having to involve higher management, so the aim is to teach them those skills. By using the Magic Questions, you can quickly assess if comments are based on Negative Impulsive Thoughts. Hopefully by this point the business will have an agreed understanding about eliminating NITs and this strategy needs to be activated.

Again, the first step is to avoid personally taking on the Negative emotion and meanwhile, "Don't react, Respond". When you are calm, you need to work out what the problem is and is there an underlying motive like malice, immaturity or a power play. Once the real problem is clear, steps can be put in place to resolve it.

Some options for peer resolution of conflict are:

- Identify this behaviour as inconsistent with the culture of the business
- Ask the person questions about the comments

- Ask the person the reasons or outcome wanted from the comments
- State that what was being said or done "seems to fall into the Negative category" (This is softer than stating the obvious facts)
- State how the comment has made you 'feel' (this is unable to be disputed)
- State what you see as the problem
- Ask if the person sees any solutions themselves
- Offer your solutions if different e.g. "Perhaps one way that would work better is to…"

Other important rules in staff conflict:

Only deal with the person concerned

The worst possible situation in business when small episodes of staff conflict occur is the ripple effect occurring through telling everyone else and not dealing with the person directly. For example, person A criticises B, B complains to C saying what a terrible person A is, C tells D and they form a little clique against A and try to pull in E, who happens to be A's best friend… Now you have all the staff attacking each other over a comment that A might have made in error or without insight. This situation could have been prevented if B directly approached A and dealt with the problem.

As a rule, staff should **only go to the staff or manager that can resolve and fix the problem**. If another staff member does not have the authority or skills to fix the problem, then they should not be involved as it causes conflict and bad attitudes in the workplace.

Do not expect to like everyone at work

The perception that you need to be 'friends' with everyone at work is absurd, because you don't choose the other staff members! What is important is that you have to be able to work together and not let any differences in lifestyle, personal attitudes, religion or behaviour interfere with your working relationship. Obviously all those issues should not interfere with effective performance at work – if it does, then the performance issues needs to be addressed and not the personal behaviours directly.

Enjoy the people at work that are your friends and be polite, charming and respectful to everyone. Maintain good working relationships with everyone you deal with and always focus on how to make the work processes better and easier for all.

Protect Your Heart

For the more sensitive amongst us, you do need to protect your heart. We have talked about the glass bubble around you where you decide what comments you let and what you let flow past. We also mentioned the Box Technique where you can place your unwanted emotional stressors and only open the box at times to suit yourself.

When there is an ongoing irritation that has penetrated your defences or is ongoing in the workplace, it is necessary to acknowledge:

- That it is out there.
- That this is the view of that person (or that they are trying to undermine you).
- You will need to deal with it in the same way as your personal NITs: Stop, Drop and Roll.

These issues of conflict do need to be controlled by you. Just ignoring them tends to allow them to ferment, stew and gain strength.

Dealing with Conflict and Aggression (physical, verbal, emotional, passive aggressive)

Aggression in workplace will usually arise from external parties like clients, related parties to clients, external contractors but also sometimes from within the workforce. The strategies in dealing with this are the same with extra control being available for employees who need to comply with the business standards.

The Key Steps in Dealing with Conflict and Aggression are:

1. Recognise escalating situations and defuse with empathy

2. Use Effective Communication – ask questions, don't prejudge, identify the problem, use paraphrasing, give simple choices, be the person to solve their problem

3. Apologise early

4. Fix the problem or work out the solution

5. Call for help/Protect yourself

Recognise an escalating situation

Aggression does not usually arise out of the blue, although this can happen. In most cases, there is a problem that the person has which they are trying to address and the responses or solution is not occurring. The increasing irritation is obvious, with increasing volume of the voice, increasingly unhappy facial expressions, reddening of the skin, and physical postures that become more threatening.

Early action at this stage can prevent the situation blowing up into shouting and physical threats. All the strategies listed above can be used and are easier at this stage because the person is still listening. Use terms like "I really want to help you so please can you explain what the problem is" or paraphrase what they have already said and feed it back to them, asking them if this is correct. Also ask them directly "What do you want from us to fix this problem?" – the sooner you can get to that point if it is possible, the sooner the situation is solved.

The most important behaviour is to avoid getting angry, annoyed or fighting back at the person in an attempt to 'defend' the business. Maintain a quiet and friendly manner, repeating the expression "I really want to help you" or "I need to get more information before we can fix this problem for you". Stating to the person "I am on your side here" also reinforces the fact that you are trying to help and when the person understands that you are his ally, his behaviour will soften. The fight back attitude just escalates the problem as it confirms that you are the enemy and the fight is on!!!

Your manner and behaviour is very important. Try to keep smiling and be pleasant. Speak softly and slowly so the person has to lower their voice and listen more carefully to hear you. Your posture needs to be open, non-aggressive and professional – you need to be perceived as not being a threat. Use of your hands can be effective to emphasise what you are saying as the person will see your mannerisms, even if they don't hear your words. Hands pushing down when asking them to lower the tone, open hands when asking questions and two hands up if you need the client to stop something.

Keep a high level of awareness of escalating anger in situations, so when you see it you can defuse it before it explodes.

Communication Strategies

It is very important to remember that behind a client complaint is the underlying feeling that the client wants to be valued and heard. Once they receive this treatment by you being attentive and empathetic to them, given their opinion important and value, it becomes easier to defuse their anger.

Effective communication is the main tool in managing aggression. The key points that you need to get across to the aggressor are that:

- You are there to help them
- You want to help them
- You want to find out what their problem is
- You will try to find solutions to the problem
- You will give them the solution they want if it is possible

If the wishes of the aggressor are not clear, some good questions to ask are – "How do you believe I can help you?"; "Do you think there is anything I can do to help solve this for you?"; "I am certainly open to trying to find a solution to this with you."; "I am here to help you."; "Please give me all the information calmly so that I am able to understand and help sort it out.".

In the early part of the discussion with an aggressive person, they are not going to listen to you much, so very short comments like these are all you might get across. They have pent-up annoyance that they may have been harbouring for days or weeks, and now they are blurting it all out. Do not try to stop this purging or interrupt them. Listen carefully and ask them questions so they are encouraged to explain exactly what has happened.

Always wait for the person to finish what they are saying without interruption, ask them several times if there was "anything else". You need them to get it all out before you start to try and address anything. Trying to step in early will not work because they are still getting their important information out and they cannot focus on anything you want to do yet.

When they have told you two or three times that there is 'nothing else' they need to tell you, you then need to paraphrase what they have said so that you summarise the story as you understand it.

The technique of paraphrasing has a number of benefits:

- It confirms to the other person that you were listening to them.
- It shows that you value what they were saying.
- It also allows you to summarise what you understand them to have said.

* It enables you to double-check that you have understood correctly.

Also in this situation, it is critical that even if you don't believe in the other person's point of view, to always acknowledge that what people say is the truth for that person at that time. Trying to argue any facts in the heat of the argument will not succeed.

Often aggression arises out of fear, and once you realise this fact it is easier to treat the person with empathy. At the end of the day, both parties want to fix the problem but as the staff member, you are the one with the skill and professionalism, so remember that the resolution has to come from you or the business.

When dealing with distressed individuals, it is also a good strategy to give them simple choices with two options. For example, "If you lower your voice, I can start to help you but if you continue to speak at me with such a loud voice, I cannot help you because we need to talk through this problem". Alternatively, be honest and say "Your manner is extremely frightening for me and I am scared. You either need to speak to me in a civilised manner or I will call the police/get you removed from the premises".

Remember your communication skills using passivity and assistance, focusing on helping the person and solving their problems, are the most powerful strategies for resolving aggressive behaviour.

Apologise Early and Fix the Problem

This has been well covered in the last sections so get practiced at working out what has upset people, apologise from that upset even if it is not your fault and look for the solution.

When you are successful at recognising the person's issues and how it affected them, you can find the reasons and offer possible solutions. Only when you successfully get the person to understand you are going to do your best to solve their problem, will you be more successful at defusing the aggressive behaviour.

Self-protection and Call for Help

1. Call for a Back-up Staff Member

   There are situations that arise where the person does not listen to reason or behave in a rational manner. If you get the feeling or sense that this person is not going to be amenable to reason or if you feel personally at risk, you do need to put steps into place to protect yourself. This may require you to get other staff members to come and observe, and your excuse for this may well be to say "Just let me go and get a more senior staff member to help us fix this problem as two heads are better than one" or a similar comment.

   Having a second staff member present only allows further help or the police to be called, but does not prevent violence from occurring. If you have anyone on staff that is male and large to provide physical protection, then they would be a good support person.

2. Move to a Private Space

   When talking to an agitated person who may present to the front desk of the business, with other customers witnessing the event, it is important to take them to an office or private setting where the matters can be sorted in private. Arrange for a second staff member to be present as a witness to prevent legal issues later and for personal protection.

3. Panic Buttons

   Depending on the type of business that you are in, the need for panic buttons may be useful. These can now be loaded on computers so that any person in any office can press the alarm and notify everyone else immediately. The traditional ones that are hard-wired are also available but require a lot more effort in installation.

4. Establish Boundaries

If the situation continues to escalate and it seems that you are not making any progress in defusing it, you need to have established boundaries that cannot be crossed. These will vary from business to business but any threats of violence, actual physical manhandling or trauma within the business are unacceptable behaviour and consequences need to result if they occur.

Explanation of the standards of the business needs to be simple and clear. For example, you can say that "In our business we treat everyone with respect and decency. Shouting, threats of violence and violence are not acceptable here. These are the standards expected of our staff and we expect the same standards from our clients as well. Therefore, if you continue to raise your voice or threaten us then we will need to end the discussion immediately and arrange to sort out the problem another day". Of course, by this time you would have used all the earlier softer strategies of trying to help the person.

Do not use the terms 'shouting' or 'aggressive' as they are judgments and the person is likely to say that they are not shouting, just using a forceful voice or they are just frustrated. The feelings of the staff member however cannot be disputed so it is fine to use terms like "Your manner is making me very scared and frightened. Behaviour like that is not acceptable in this facility/business as our standards are that everyone should be respected and feel safe without fear".

Another strategy to use at this late stage is to offer the person to "come back tomorrow when you have had a chance to calm down so everyone can work together to find a solution to the problem". An organised appointment time and office booked for the purpose and the "appropriate managers and senior staff can be there to address the important issues". This gives the business the time to investigate the issue as well and decide on the solutions that can be offered.

5. Call the Police:

This is the last straw but if the behaviour is unrelenting and continues to be unacceptable then it needs to be done. The second staff member can use the phone while the conversation continues with the aggressor. Before this occurs, the warnings should be given again "If you do not lower your voice, we will call the police", or "Please settle down so that we can help you but if this behaviour does not stop, we will need to have you removed and will call the police".

Summary

Positively managing conflict, complaints and aggression requires these steps:

1.   Focus on complaints as learning tools

2.   Take 100% responsibility and apologise early

3.   Fix the problem fast

4.   Focus on the problem, not the person

5.   Don't React, Respond

6.   Communicate with listening, paraphrasing and be on their side

7.   Establish boundaries

8.   Maintain a class act

CHAPTER 5

The 'Business Tree' Analogy

CHAPTER 5

The 'Business Tree' Analogy

"When you are exceptional, you jump off the page. Take the high road – it's far less crowded!"

– Warren Buffet

Our years of experience in business organisations from small to large led us to the realisation that many employees did not keep the business's best interests and financial viability in mind during everyday operations. The staff often see the business as a huge profit-making entity that is unaffected by what they do as single individuals. The result is that staff have little or no regards for the finer details within the business and sometimes do not care about efficiency, productivity and maintenance of business income or limitation of business costs.

Even worse, staff will take unapproved products, services or time directly from the business, even though in reality this is theft. The result spells potential disaster for the business if the viability is being attacked from all sides by staff. The irony is that their future employment is completely dependent on working in a sustainable business, and that is what they are undermining!

This problem resulted in our creation of the 'Business Tree' analogy. The principle is that the business is like a tree that was planted by the owners as a seed, was nurtured for some time while it was unproductive and has grown up over time to become bigger and stronger. As the tree has grown, more and more animals make it their home, using it for their housing and for food from the fruits or leaves. Some animals live in the tree like birds and squirrels but other animals live under the tree and catch the falling fruit. The animals that live off the production of the tree are like the workers or employees of business. As the tree grows larger, there are more and more animals that receive benefits from the tree and are dependent on its health.

Throughout the life of the tree there are 'guardians' of the tree that are responsible for making sure the tree prospers and grows. They are responsible for the health of the tree and are there to protect the tree, making sure that nothing bad happens that will restrict the benefits of the tree like wood rot, disease of the leaves, digging up of the roots or cutting off of the limbs. The guardians of the tree are the managers, supervisors or owner of the business.

For the tree (business) to prosper, it needs to be getting enough fertiliser, water and sunshine. For the tree to flourish, it needs to be growing faster than it is being cut back. So every animal in the tree that is taking fruits or leaves (money or products) from the tree is undermining future growth and while each animal thinks that they are not doing any harm, add up all the animals taking what they should not and there could be a problem.

Next, we need to consider some other types of activities – the woodpecker that is drilling holes in the trunk and may destroy the fundamental structure of the tree. The animals that are digging out the roots of the tree to eat the truffles underneath can also result in the death of the tree in the next storm as it gets blown over. A large animal like an elephant may come along and completely knock it over so the guardians' role is to protect the tree from all risks.

Inadequate nutrients for the tree will result in deficiency problems and all the leaves may fall off. A variety of diseases can occur to the tree, any of which will reduce the productivity or death of the tree.

If everyone loves the tree and looks after it, the tree will flourish providing housing and food for all the animals and birds associated with it. However, if the tree is progressively stripped or undermined so that it can't survive, then all the animals lose their homes, food and their benefits.

Risks to the 'Business Tree'

Lots of little animals stripping leaves or branches off the tree will kill it just as effectively as the elephant coming along and knocking it over. Examples of business stripping would be the wasting, stealing or 'borrowing' of business property, clothing, money or products. The excess claiming of expenses may seem a small amount to the single employee but multiply that out by all the employees and viability may be affected.

The woodpecker chipping away at the trunk could be workers that are being negative to major customers about the business so they go elsewhere. Some staff may be effectively cutting off whole limbs of the tree if they want to set up in competition and take those clients with them.

Internal rot in the trunk or wood could be considered to be negativity and internal squabbling within in the staff. If it gets severe enough, the rot will result in the tree falling apart so needs to be recognised and treated early.

The guardians of the tree are the ones that are given the responsibility of looking after the tree and watching for early sign of any of these risks from inside or outside. They need to respond early, remove the risks and repair any damage that has occurred.

Every animal that is getting benefit from the tree will suffer if the tree is not productive. At the same time, the tree cannot be productive if all the animals are not working in unison for the good of the tree. It is a mutually beneficial process and animals at all levels need to be on the side of benefiting the tree if the tree will be able to provide benefits back to the animals.

In exactly the same way, all workers need to be working for the benefit of the business so that the business can continue to provide housing, food and money for the workers. If the workers at the different levels are undermining the business in many small ways, the business will be compromised – and all the workers will lose their jobs if the business falls over!

Change in Workers Attitude to the 'Business Tree'

This 'Business Tree' analogy allows workers to understand that they need to working for the benefit of the business and not just taking whatever they can. Undermining the business will lead to failure – every lost dollar of income, dollar lost or spent unnecessarily, money or products stolen or wasted makes a difference. The analogy also gives managers a clearer view of their role and this analogy has the power to change people's perception for the better about their relationship to the business that employs them.

Understanding of this tree analogy also gives the business owners and managers the ability to remove themselves personally from decisions that often have to be made in the course of a day. Extra pressure is often put on the business owner, which often takes the form of the employees asking for more out of the business. This can be in the form of a pay increase, extra personal expenses, non-essential business purchases (that an employee considers a good idea) or perhaps unauthorised 'borrowing' and non-return of items. It can be an ongoing process because the owners and managers need to be constantly vigilant as they are the ultimate guardians of the 'tree'.

It is important that the employees are made aware of the tree analogy and this can be effectively achieved in a one hour staff meeting. The relevant areas to your business can be highlighted in that meeting to have the greatest immediate impact and then reinforced over time. This principle can also be used for discussions with individual staff members in disciplinary processes or problem solving. The message does need to get out to all staff members at all levels in the business to establish the principle and then reinforcement of the principle used when good examples arise.

Rules of Change – Approval for Change Processes

Before staff members make any decision to change established processes in the business, there are three questions that they must ask themselves and these are called the 'Rules of Change':

1. Will this decision/action benefit the 'Tree'?
2. Will the decision/action benefit others?
3. Will this decision/action compromise the 'Tree' in any way?

Obviously, if the answer to Question 1 is 'yes' and the Tree benefits, it is a no-brainer. If the Tree will 'NOT' benefit from the change, then, who will be the beneficiary? This spotlights the possibility of the staff member performing actions for their benefit or other parties external to the business. Clearly if that is the case, further investigation is required. If the Tree will be compromised in any way, that should be revealed by Question 3. Again that makes the decision easy and the action should not be done.

These three questions make is very easy to assess proposed changes and whether they should be followed through or rejected, because the focus is on the best interests of the "Tree". The business owner or manager is also personally distanced from any rejected request as the focus remains the best interest of the business and would not be expected to make poor business decisions.

Educating your employees to ask these questions before they take action or make a business decision minimises losses and errors of judgment. However, it still allows employees to take initiative within that structure and avoids the owners or managers having to micromanage their employees.

In the event that a suggestion is rejected, another great tactic is to place the responsibility back to the person requesting the change to come up with an alternative solution. The aim is to produce the positive change that they seek and at the same time creating a positive (or neutral) outcome for the Tree resulting in a win–win situation. This also teaches your staff to think more broadly and over time they will only come to you with the win–win solutions already worked out.

Real Life Example

Many years ago we learnt a valuable lesson as our company expanded internationally and more staff and managers joined our organisation. An interesting situation developed with our resort business in Indonesia, where we had developed the best and most authentic day spa on an exotic island. Being a trainer of spa therapists, I created an amazing service menu, spent months sourcing the finest spa products to deliver high quality for our customers, and trained all our staff.

John and I designed and built a beautiful spa from nothing, following Feng Shui principles, down to details like sculptured fountains in a huge pond, flowing water, fish and turtles. Every detail was considered and it was an amazing success.

Due to a lack of experienced managers locally, we were forced to employ managers who had no knowledge in the spa field. We trained and coached them to the level that was satisfactory to maintain standards and the status quo of the spa. Just over 12 months into one of our new manager's role, I returned to our resort and was utterly surprised to find that all of the natural product I had sourced had been replaced with a very low quality product with a cheap chemical odour.

Investigation revealed that the new manager had now started his own wholesale spa product business on the side (while still working for us) and had our spa buying all of his cheap products instead of the ones that I had chosen.

We approached this with positivity and asked him to explain why this had occurred using the 'first ask questions' principle. It did not occur to him he should have discussed the change, let alone get authority for this action that had the potential to destroy the quality and integrity of our spa.

He had no idea what chemicals were in his products or what side effects they could have on people's skin or bodies. Clearly it was a case of personal profiteering without any consideration of the benefits or risks to the business. If we had of had the 'Rules of Change' in place, he would have first had a discussion with us before making such a significant change and a better outcome for the business would have been considered!

"Will this action benefit the business?" – clearly not. But I would have responded by saying "If you, as a wholesaler, can find a better, natural product than the ones we are currently using that costs cost less, I would consider taking a look and testing it and perhaps making the change".

Clearly the "tree analogy" and "Rules of Change" would have saved this situation from snowballing. However, we now look back and feel grateful for these jewels of wisdom that the situation taught us. Every business can benefit from this safety net and use this principle to clearly establish the benefits and risks of all actions, from minor personal actions to major business decisions. This process can be easily implemented in any business so you can take advantage of these effective techniques.

Summary

Establishing a business can be compared to the planting of a seedling and it growing into a huge tree. When nurtured and tended well, it grows and flourishes. If it is stripped, undermined, diseased, undernourished or not cared for, it will wither and die.

In exactly the same way, businesses rely on all their workers to support and grow the business, not undermine and strip its assets or profitability. Both the tree and businesses will come tumbling down if they are not cared for, loved, protected, nurtured and positively supported by all involved.

Use the 'Rules of Change' questions to assess all new actions and decisions in the business. This will easily highlight if, who and where the benefits are received and if the action is good for the business. All new decisions and actions should go through this quick assessment before they are implemented.

CHAPTER 6

How to Hire and Retain Fantastic Staff

CHAPTER 6

How to Hire and Retain Fantastic Staff

"Be mindful of the power of your words. Be part of the reason someone succeeded, not part of the reason they failed."

– Eli McIntosh

Let's go back to imagining a business that is a pleasure to be a part of, where every employee is happy to be there, with a positive 'can-do' attitude. How great would it be to have no interpersonal conflict, backbiting or denigration in the workplace? This is achievable and the benefits are significant at all levels of operations to profitability.

There are two sides to this process – the first is to develop strategies to make sure you hire the right people, and secondly you need to make sure that you retain the good staff. Businesses often lose good staff because of the negative actions taken by others in the workplace or because of a toxic atmosphere.

How much time, money and energy is wasted on low level, day to day interpersonal staff issues that have no direct benefit on productivity in your business? This is the 80% hassle factor that does not contribute to profits as described in the 80/20 rule. Eliminate or dramatically reduce this major non-productive element in your time management and the managers and owners can focus their efforts at productivity and profits. Processes for hiring and retaining the right people will be explained in this chapter.

It doesn't matter the nature of the business, as the principles remain the same.

As employers, we want the best skilled staff to work for our business and unfortunately some of those people with the right skills will have the wrong attitudes. A person with great skills but a poor attitude can cause immense damage to the organisation, despite the skills that they bring. A single employee with a negative attitude can undermine and destroy the team cohesion, productivity and the whole workplace environment that they are in.

Therefore, the importance of hiring the right staff for your business cannot be emphasised enough, as it can mean the difference between business growth or stagnation, progress and resistance, and ultimately success or failure.

We have heard it said many times that the hardest thing to manage in business is the people and it absorbs inappropriately large amounts of time. As business managers, we do have a choice to either continue being distracted by interpersonal conflict, staffing issues and stamping out fires, or we can take back control to set high standards of conduct.

The processes that we are spotlighting here have benefits at multiple levels from hiring good skilled staff with good attitudes, to reinforcing a good workplace atmosphere, a great culture, better customer service and profits. There are also the soft benefits like improved work satisfaction which leads to staff retention, and staff that are willing to go the extra mile for the business. It does all start at the recruitment and hiring steps to eliminate negative elements from your business and drive it towards positivity in all areas.

Section 1 – The Five-Step Interview Process

Like many large organisations, our company has branches nationally and internationally and ranges across many different industries, from medical to property development, hospitality, publishing, beauty, industrial innovation and charter businesses.

Having gone through the process of hiring new staff over many years using the traditional interviewing processes, the true nature of the candidates was usually hidden in the interview facade. It was like playing Russian roulette as the true personal attitudes are usually never fully disclosed and you never knew which employee would cause trouble later and 'explode' in some way!

As a result, we developed a unique approach that placed us back in the control seat and gave us the ability to assess true applicant potential. This also gives protection for the business should the applicants performance be lower than that stated in the interview process. The 5-Step Interview Process is explained here. This process assumes that you have separately assessed the skills of the person as being appropriate and now you are trying to assess if their attitude is appropriate for employment.

Step ❶ Ensuring Applicant is a 'Cultural Fit' (Use your Culture Statements)

A useful opening to explain the organisation's position is to ask questions about how the applicant has prepared for the interview. Have they checked your website or Facebook pages and what do they know about you and your organisation? Do they know anything about the business's expectations in service levels and its positive culture?

The answers to these questions will tell you a lot about the person you are considering hiring, if they are conscientious, organised, prepared and investigative. The questions also open up the opportunity to move into the explanation about the importance of your positive culture and then move into details to describe your Culture Statements. It needs to be clear that these are established standards of behaviour and performance that are universal and mandatory.

At this point in our interviews a printed version of our Culture Statement is given to the applicant and the key points are discussed one by one. The body language of the applicant needs to be observed for enthusiastic agreement or an internal struggle with the positive culture. If someone is struggling with the concepts they will usually not verbalise any resistance but you will notice signs of discomfort, agitation, confusion, concern, frowning and crossing the arms.

On the other hand, if the person is enthusiastic about the Culture Statements, they are likely to enthusiastically express how they approve and make statements like "This is great – I wish we had these at my last workplace!" The nonverbal signals you will notice will be eyes widening, straightening of posture, more rapid breathing, excitement in the tone, usually a little higher pitch, speaking faster and increased excited body movements. Usually the applicant also gives examples of good or negative work experiences to illustrate they are in agreement and are excited at such a positive culture.

The supportive applicant clearly understands what your culture is striving for, and is eager to work in such an environment and this means that they are in alignment with your culture already.

At this point, you can discuss in more detail how to be solution-focused, taking personalities out of the mistakes, and coming to your manager with solutions, not problems. You can explain further important aspects of the Culture Statements that relate to their position and what won't be tolerated in your business, like gossip, backbiting, blaming and denigration.

Establishing the standards of the business and the Culture Statement at this point is essential and worth the extra time involved as it legally and clearly documents the requirements of the business and the applicant's acceptance of those standards. This is reinforced as the new employee also signs their agreement to the Culture Statements as part of the employment contract paperwork.

Step ② Explain that Employees take 100% Responsibility

Every employee being 100% responsible for the outcomes of their actions has such value that it should be specifically mentioned in the interview process. It should be noted that two of the Culture Statements refer to the 100% Responsibility principle – Ownership and Communication:

Ownership *– I take full responsibility for all of my actions, words, outcomes and all that takes place in my life.*

Communication *– I always speak positively of my fellow team members, clients, doctors and the practice in both public and private. All my words are for good purpose, using positive and empowering terms. I do not use or listen to gossip, profanity, sarcasm or derogatory language and I will only speak constructively. I greet and farewell people using their names **and take responsibility for responses to my communication.***

Taking responsibility for personal actions is covered by the first statement to avoid the 'ripple effect' of damage and conflict spreading because of trying to pass responsibility for mistakes to others. Taking responsibility for communications is covered in the second statement and this reinforces that it is each person's responsibility to ensure that what they have said is understood or will be acted upon appropriately by the other party. It is not enough just to say what is needed, it is essential that the understanding of what you have said is correct.

The management of mistakes is covered in more detail in another chapter but is based on acknowledging the mistake early, apologising and fixing the problem fast.

Step ❸ Establish the Conflict Resolution Process

Throughout the interview, it is a good strategy to discuss the key problems that the business faces regularly, and explain how the employees are expected to behave or act under those circumstances. One of the most common problems is that of communication breakdown or interpersonal conflict and the expected behaviours needs to be explained.

For example, if a staff member wants to know something, they ask the person who has the correct answer or has the authority to determine the correct answer. Problems will often arise if they ask their co-worker who has only a vague idea and then may give incorrect information. The passing on of inaccurate information from one worker to another results in progressively poor practices and establishment of improper procedures as the status quo. Obviously work instructions or Business Protocols should be in place to answer most questions, so refer to them as well.

If a staff member has an issue with someone, they discuss with that person directly as they are the person that can clear it up, as discussed in Chapter 4. If that direct approach does not work and the matter needs to be resolved, then the issue needs to be taken to the immediate supervisor or manager and progress the issue to more senior staff.

The other flow on issue is that of who to approach if an employee needs something resolved by anyone including management. The principle here is also that it should only be discussed with the person who can solve your problem and not with anyone else. So, if there is a roster issue, talk to the manager or roster master, if there is a pay or superannuation issue, talk to the accounts department. If the matter is discussed with co-workers, it becomes gossip and can cause confusion, undermining the positive culture. Often there is no error, but a misunderstanding by the employee, so having them saying that the "company is not paying me correctly" undermines trust for everyone.

At this point you should ask to have some feedback from the applicant for further confirmation that they understand the concept of positive culture. They are also asked to confirm that they can embrace this work culture, as they will be required to agree to this when they sign the companies work agreement contract.

Step ④ The 'Best Version of You' Talk

The next important topic to discuss at the interview is that, if they are awarded the job position, the person who is being employed is the one who is sitting across the table now at this interview. You need to lay it on the line and tell them "The person who we are looking to employ in front of us now is immaculately dressed, enthusiastic, attentive, flexible, with a can-do attitude, is solution focused, conscientious and has agreed to live by our positive culture.

"It is this 'Best Version of You' that we are employing today and that is exactly who I expect to present for work every day. Do you understand what I mean by this and can we expect you to live up to everything you have told us today on an ongoing basis?" It is important that there is no confusion of the quality, class and expectation of the person who is taking the job."

This places the responsibility right in their lap to perform to the expected level. At any stage, if the employee is underperforming, they can be reminded that their employment was based on them maintaining the 'best version of themselves every day. You then ask them, what steps do they think they have to take to ensure that their 'best version' is maintained as per your employment agreement.

Since we implemented this strategy, there has been a dramatic reduction in the ongoing issues that we face. When conversations are needed with staff about their attitude, all the emotion and uncomfortable awkwardness that accompanies these types of conversation is avoided and the matter is simplified enormously. "These are the standards that you agreed to and are not conforming with what you promised. What steps are you going to take to fix this problem and that will allow me to restore my confidence that you will perform the requirements of the position to the expected level?"

Step ⑤ The 'Balanced Relationship' Talk

The 'Balanced Relationship' talk is the last major discussion to have at the interview process. The principle is that as employer and employee, we form a relationship in the form of a contract. The business promises to provide reward in the form of wages at the end of the week, it gives its written word that it will keep its part of the agreement as per the contract, and the employee agrees to provide their ongoing work and positive conduct in the business.

The applicant needs to know for any relationship to work and flourish, both parties need to commit to each other and have a balanced and fair relationship. When one party gives constantly and the other takes, the giving party will eventually become disenchanted and the relationship breaks down. The giver can be either the business or the employee but a healthy balance must be maintained for the longevity of the relationship.

It is useful to give examples of giving and taking on both sides – the business may need extra from the employee at times with flexibility of hours, location, cross covering others position temporarily or extended responsibility.

There will be times that the business will give willingly in the form of special events, time-off given, flexibility, added benefits, discounts, free benefits, training, gifts of appreciation. For the 'Balanced Relationship' to be maintained, it should not always be the same party (employer or employee) that is giving the extra and paying the extra price. If the relationship becomes unbalanced, one party will become disgruntled and the parties will separate.

Again, if all these issues are address and understood by all at the start of the relationship, there will be fewer surprises and situations that occur down the road that results in either of the parties becoming disgruntled. It also provides an avenue for future discussions from either party when pay rates and rewards are being discussed.

When all these five steps have been taken in the interview process and the Culture Statement signed as part of the employment contract, a Positive Cultural expectation is established for both parties. The parameters are established legally that protect the business should behaviour stray from the desired path and give the business the standards to fall back on should dispute resolution situations arise. This level of detail is very infrequently included in work contracts but is critical for creation of a Positive Workplace Culture and atmosphere.

Establishing these parameters also allows the prospective employees to have a clear understanding of what is expected, the boundaries and what is not tolerated. This saves an enormous amount of trouble, time, emotion, money and effort in the future when staff issues or problems arise.

Section 2 – The Five Steps to Retaining Fantastic Staff

Having employed staff with the strategies above, it is also important to make sure that the fantastic staff that are positive and supportive are retained in the long term. It is certainly more cost effective to invest in the retention of the good staff for the long term as the employment and orientation process for new staff is a major cost to the business. So here are steps to put in place to ensure maximum staff retention levels and how to use your Positive Culture to maximise both longevity of staff but also to reduce sick days, absenteeism and presenteeism (underperforming at work).

Step ❶ Value and Recognition of Staff

Recognition of staff members for their effort at work is as important as the wages they receive. In some cases, the recognition is more important than the money and from the business owner's perspective, this is very important to recognise as you can get huge benefits from putting in place a structured staff recognition process with relatively little expense.

Staff Awards and Prizes

Common examples of staff recognition processes include 'Employee of the Month' where the employee is chosen every month and given the label and recognition. It is important for this recognition to be performed in front of all co-workers and preferably in a staff meeting. Giving details of why that person was chosen for the award is also important so that all the other staff members know what the person has done and how they have stepped above the normal to achieve the award.

Along with any award may come a prize that can be a token of some kind for movies, a meal, a trip or a treatment of some kind. The value is less important than the recognition so it is better to hand out regular awards more frequently with less value than once a year with larger values.

High value gifts can be useful for more senior staff in a large organisation to help motivate the other senior staff. Having the high value awards being unpredictable and performance-based rather than time-based is useful in avoiding predictability of knowing that an award is due and staff changing their behaviour artificially and temporarily for it.

A typical process that we have found to be successful is to present three awards monthly to a workplace of about sixty people where they are recognised in front of everyone and their extra value efforts described. They have their photo up in the waiting room for the month, on Facebook and the website and receive two movie tickets, facials, massages or meal vouchers! This event is quite moving and we have had staff members in tears of happiness as a result of their recognition and true appreciation of their effort!

Performance-Based Awards

It is possible to create performance-based awards that are openly calculated on sales, turnover or profits. As these are predictable, they are usually considered by the staff as work bonuses that they work towards, rather than being given for outstanding actions. They are useful if their presence will increase performance and maintain higher levels of sales figures but if there is less emotional value on them, they do not have the same positive effect as the recognition awards of effort for excellence and will often cost more money.

Public Promotion of Awards

Employee of the month awards are commonly placed as photos in the common areas of the workplace. With the internet and social media, it is also important to post these awards on Facebook pages and your business website. Having your business keeping your website and social media sites active and regularly changing is important so that more individuals see the awards and the positive feedback gets back to the winners.

Responsibilities for Social Activities

Some staff members receive personal value from functioning as social conveners or organising events that are required by the business or charity events. Supporting the community and charities is an important function for all businesses and that time that the employee contributes is usually only partly funded by the business as much time is usually also spent after hours.

The individual achieves improved status, recognition and respect as the organiser, even though there is probably a lot of their time that they have contributed for free.

Step ❷ Create Job Satisfaction and Career Progression

Job satisfaction means different things to different people so as the business owner or manager, it is important to know what each person's ideal job and long term goals are. Some will just want to work in the position they are applying for or in and some are looking for career or skills advancement. To maintain a happy workforce, knowing the long-term goals of your employees is important. That knowledge allows you to give some a career path and others are happy to stay put. You will also know that for those that you can't give any advancement, they are likely to be moving on at some point.

Regular review of goals and career aspirations can be discussed at the annual performance reviews. Even for those individuals that will stay with your business forever, developing and advancing their skills in different areas will result in them staying with you for longer so there are advantages in being creative to see how every staff members' goals can be assisted within your business.

Even for those employees that have no desire to rise in the career path may have interests in doing other aspects of the business and it is important to ensure that the individuals are not getting bored or lacking work stimulation.

Step ③ Regular Review of Goals (annual performance)

While the annual performance review is traditionally used to assess the workers' performance against the business' requirements, it is a very useful time for the manager or owner to ask general questions about the person and the business functioning. This assessment is usually stressful for the staff so they often approach it with fear and just want to get it over with. Moving past this fear is essential before any honest feedback can be obtained.

The extra areas of interest to ask about (other than the actual performance criteria) are to ask about the employee personally, their goals, the business atmosphere and any areas where things can be improved. The least challenging of these is how they find the business is running, the level of positivity in the workplace and how they see the team is operating as a group. Ask if there are any areas in the business (or their area) that they see could be improved and to reinforce that if they have any constructive suggestions to bring them forward.

To address the personal areas (you have already dealt with their personal performance assessment), you can ask how they are personally finding their working environment and if there are any areas that reduce their effectiveness how they are going in the business. What are their long-term goals and are they making progress towards them? Is there anything that could be done in the business to assist them in the process?

By taking a real interest in each person's personal goals and using the business as a tool for advancing employees' careers, creates loyalty and dedication that is often returned in ways that money cannot buy.

This interest in individual's personal dreams and goals led us to encouraging one worker to follow her dream to study medicine at the age of 40 years old. We encouraged and assisted her through the preliminary stages until she was accepted and obviously at that point we lost her as a worker. But we are rewarded with the joy of knowing that she is living her dream and achieving what she really wanted to do!

Step ④ Allow Innovative Thinking for New Solutions

The creation of a stimulating work environment that is rewarding and interesting for all of our staff members has always been our goal. Creating an environment where innovative solutions to provide solutions to everyday problems creates the intellectual stimulation and is very effective at improving staff retention. This process has two benefits – if gives the creative thinkers an avenue to explore better ways of getting their work done, along with the recognition of their innovative solution and those improved systems make everyone's work environment better and easier!

Every workplace has a potential brain bank that increases with every extra staff member. Use this brain bank to find new solutions to problems using the staff that are best at performing that task. By allowing free thought and creativity, the interest in the job can be improved even though there is repetition.

When new processes are suggested and a trial of the process is proposed, we try to use the creator to institute the trial if that is possible. That way, the driver of the process is the creator and they are going to be the most motivated person in relation to the process. If the trial is successful, the processes are spread across the organisation and that person is given full credit for their ingenuity publicly (as in the awards section).

It is important to recognise that innovative solutions need to be searched for by workers at every level of the business as it is absurd to imagine that the senior staff could see technical inefficiencies on the shop floor. Therefore, innovation and improved systems are everyone's responsibility.

Step ⑤ Eli Mc's Applauding Outstanding Performance

Here is an extremely effective process for improving individual self-value and pride in your workforce. The process works in the workplace, in sports teams and groups of any kind. It is a process created by Elizabeth McIntosh and has dramatic effects with the positive feedback and emotional connection that usually results.

The exercise takes place during a staff meeting or presentation and each staff member is given post-it notes with the names of the main workers with whom they have direct contact at the start of the meeting. There is one name on each piece of paper and each person is given 5–10 notes. Each staff member is then required to write one word or a short phrase about what they admire or have noticed that is positive or outstanding for each person. They should write the single most impressive feature in that word or phrase and not put the writer's name on the paper.

These instructions are given at the start of the staff meeting and each person is given time during the meeting to think about each person and fill in the details of their people during the next 30 minutes. They are reminded to fill in the notes through the meeting and given a few minutes at the end if there are any notes not completed.

With at least 20 minutes left of the meeting time, each post-it note is then collected and separated into each person's list so staff members have 5-10 sheets relating to them. Each individual is then asked to stand up and read out what others acknowledge as their outstanding features.

There are times that staff are so emotional that they are not able to read out their compliments and the exercise has everyone leaving on an incredible emotional high. The beauty of the process is also that while you feel wonderful about what others have said about you, you also feel wonderful for the congratulations that each other person receives as well.

The key to this exercise seems to be that when things go wrong we tell each other quickly but for the rest of the time, we do not compliment and congratulate each other much at all. This exercise reinforces the positive values and skills that each of us has and the repetition from the multiple comments shows that the compliments are true and heart felt.

This exercise is unbelievably uplifting for the soul and humbling for everyone. It brings people so much closer together and often brings people to tears. It is very effective at team building and recommended for every workplace!

Summary

Quality staff are the key to great workplace and an effective team. The interview process can establish the expected culture, work performance levels and the principles of taking 100% responsibility. Follow that with the processes for conflict resolution, the 'Best Version of You' and 'Balanced Relationship' talks and you have the basis for obtaining the fantastic staff.

Retaining these staff requires staff to feel recognised, valued and appreciated. Know and review their career goals and aspirations and fulfil these as much as possible. Allow the workplace to have innovative and creative thinking for improvement and perform 'Eli Mc's Applauding Outstanding Performance' exercise for amazing results in team building.

Ten Psychological Tips for Outstanding Customer Service

CHAPTER 7

Ten Psychological Tips for Outstanding Customer Service

"Your most unhappy customers are your greatest source of learning."

– Bill Gates

A great company's mission should be always aiming to deliver the best service and product it can. There should be a continuous process in every business to search for ways to improve standards and services in your industry, in order to consistently place your business in front of your competitors. Customer service is the most critical area as this is what creates and retains your income base.

It is imperative that all of your staff know and operate with the Positive Culture standards that have been set and then also use these psychological tips with customers whenever possible. This way the company will ensure consistent quality control and every customer will have the same high quality experience as the next.

These tips when used correctly are extremely powerful tools of persuasion and in business this is one the most significant attributes you and your every member of your staff can possess. Everyone that walks the planet wants to sell something to someone, whether you work in sales or not – we are selling ourselves every time we apply for a job, offer to provide a service or even when we are socialising and trying to make friends. In business, every day we are promoting ourselves, our business, our services and our ability to deliver.

The secret to 'selling' is learning to achieve great rapport, and have an understanding of how it works in practical terms. Rapport is based on understanding human behaviour at a psychological level, what makes us do things, how we feel when we are speaking to someone, and what compels us to use a service or make a purchase.

Rapport works on the basis that we, as human beings will do things for others, or purchase from your company, if people like you. If they like you, they will tend to trust you and where there is trust, there are sales. Rapport is based on aiming to be 'in sync' with someone because the more someone knows we are like them, the more they will trust us. This is done in numerous ways however the most basic is focused on body language.

Mimicking (subtly) how they are sitting, for instance legs crossed, arms folded etc., if they move you move. Politicians and celebrities are often well-versed in rapport where it is possible to be in opposition or someone being opposed to an idea and a great rapport artist can not only break through this resistance but can convert them to a believer. We teach this skill to businesses with amazing results, not only in business but in personal lives also.

These ten psychological tricks are based on some those principles of rapport and even though we could write a whole book just on the subject of rapport, our aim was to give you a brief overview and some great techniques to hugely improve your service.

The effects are immense and you can make a difference just by using the *key words* with your customers, understanding their key motivating factors or phrasing things in certain ways can make the difference to make that appointment or closing that sale. Every appointment or contact made is gold as one lead can have a domino effect that could translate into thousands of dollars to your company from that one person.

1 Introduce yourself by your 'name'

Names are an important part of rapport as they bridge many boundaries at a psychological level. Therefore, introduce yourself with your own name and in such a way that the person can hear it clearly and repeat it later in the discussion. The client then relates to you as a person, a friend and someone they can trust.

While normal manners and protocols would expect an introduction to occur, reinforce your name later in the conversation by repeating it, for example by saying "If you need any assistance with the product afterwards, just ask to speak to me, *Jo Bloggs*" or "If you need any information in the future, my name is *Jo Bloggs* so you can ask for me".

There is an underlying confidence that if at any time after they have committed to your service or product if they are not getting what they should have, that you will help them get it sorted as they know your name and they know you personally.

2 Use the customer's name three times in every contact with them

The next important technique in building rapport and trust is to learn your customer's name and use it 3 times in your first meeting and every time after that. This results in the client feeling at ease and a relationship of trust, like a friend, is started between two individuals. This use of the client's name is also important to be used when attempting to handle any complaint that they may have.

For example, you may say "Joanne, let me say to you right now that we are sorry you feel so upset and that this has happened. Also let me promise you, Joanne that I will do all I can to help sort this out for you now. Are you willing to work with me to find a solution to resolve the problem for you, Joanne?"

③ Use key words like 'when' or 'how'

Using the right words that will lead to appointments, sales, a contract or deal can be an art that comes naturally or a skill that you need to learn. "That guy just seems to be able to sell anything – he just has a way with words" is sometimes heard and there is more truth in that saying than people realise. What 'that guy' has learned is that when you phrase your sentences in a certain way, it makes it difficult for people to say 'no' or refuse. If you want everyone to start giving you positive responses to your offers, do not give them an easy option of saying 'no'.

The way to achieve this is to say *"When* would you like to make that appointment?" and not "Would you like to make an appointment?" The use of "when" implies that the person already wants to make an appointment and is more difficult to refuse.

Also, when someone walks into your business, your staff should ask *"How* can I help you?" instead of "Can I help you?" and implies that the staff person can help them in some way. Asking "How" will lead a conversation that will answer the question and the customer will often share their confusion or what is on their mind and allow the sales person to help them.

Using the terms "when" and "how" in questions avoids using questions where the reply could be a "yes" or a "no", and leads to a more in-depth conversation that is more likely to lead to a sale.

4 Don't let the phone ring more than three times before answering

Everyone is time-poor these days and when we phone businesses it can be very frustrating having to wait for long periods to get through. This is especially true when you are trying to use their services and give them work. Failure to answer the phone sends out a number of psychological messages to customers – is the business understaffed, are they unable to provide efficient services or don't they value their customers enough to keep them waiting that long? As the phone call lengthens, the spiral of doubts and loss of confidence in that business escalates to the point that the customer may choose to go elsewhere and call your competition!

This simple act of efficient phone etiquette is so much more important to the business than most telephonists and receptionists understand – it remains a high priority – so answer the phone within three rings!

In the event that you are unable to fully deal with the call immediately, it is still better to answer the call, ensure it is not a critical emergency and put the person on hold until you can get back to them. Then apologise for any delay and deal with their enquiry.

⑤ Greet everyone that walks through the door *quickly* and with a *smile*

Although this is so obvious and simple, it is so often forgotten. The receptionist is usually very busy and the pressures of work can be high. It is a frequent and quite insulting process to be waiting at a front counter with a staff member right in front of you who is busy with paperwork or on the phone and you get completely ignored. The message that the customer is getting is that they are not important, not valued and perhaps a bit of a nuisance. In reality, it is the customers that are paying for the wages of all the staff so they need to feel as they are the most important people around.

Therefore, acknowledge the customer with a large smile and introduction as soon as the approach the desk. In the situations that the staff member is tied up with a phone call or another person, acknowledge them with your eyes, a smile and a gesture that they will be served after the call or that you will be with them in a minute. You will find customers are happy to wait if you acknowledge them.

The psychological messages that this sends to your customer is that I know that you are here, I value your custom and I want you to know I will do my best to attend to you as soon as possible.

The other aspect of this first encounter is that the front desk staff need to portraying an air of friendly, fast efficiency. It is fine for the staff to be busy or even very busy but it is not acceptable to be portraying stress, agitation, annoyance, not coping or being frazzled. The message this sends to the customers is obviously negative with the implication of being out of control, poorly organised, chaotic and unprofessional. Therefore, no matter what the degree of chaos that is occurring in the business, like swans, staff should maintain the visible signs of smooth and efficient professionalism while underneath they may be paddling like crazy!

Most of us have all had some kind of experience of seeing the chaotic front desk staff with the person clearly frazzled, stressed and annoyed at her level of work. Even worse if she then proceeds to tell you how she is struggling on her own, making the customer feel so bad for being such an inconvenience. In one situation like this I have even offered to answer the phone for her to help her out!

Ensure that your staff never behaves like this and if they still don't understand the powerful messages the front desk person can give out, perhaps they are better working in back office! Aim for every customer to be dealt with promptly with a smile with the whole atmosphere being professional, calm and efficient even if it is busy and high-pressure events that are occurring.

6 Always have a smile on your face when speaking on the phone

When someone is speaking with a smile on their face, the words sound different. As well as this, the speaker tends to use a lighter tone that comes across as pleasant and easy to deal with. As strange as it may sound, customers can tell the difference in your voice when you are talking with a smile on your face. Customers are very perceptive with senses out like antennas picking up all they can from the conversation, even on a subconscious level.

On a psychological level, even if your staff has to 'pretend' to be happy when they pick up the phone, at the end of the phone call they will actually feel happier. This is a proven phenomenon!

❼ Call the customer on the next business day for a follow up after a service or purchase for satisfaction feedback

This is not common practice in our business world today given our fast pace, and pressure to move on to the next customer. As a result, this has even more impact and this level of customer service speaks volumes. This courtesy call tells your customers you value them, that you want to ensure they are happy with their purchase or service, they managed to get it working, all the parts were there and that they will use you again or recommend to a friend. It boosts loyalty to your brand and reinforces your service as being superior to your competition.

If you weigh up how much money business spends on advertising to get new business on an ongoing basis, the small cost and time that is used to add satisfaction to an existing customer is incomparable. They are much more likely to use you again next time, plus they will be so impressed that they will have no hesitation in recommending your business to a friend. Word of mouth is the best form of advertising you can invest in and the most effective!

❽ Give people two choices of action, not choice of action or no action

Whatever product of service a customer is looking at, phrase any questions around which one of the services would they prefer with a choice of two or more. "Would you prefer this design or that one?" or "Would you prefer this colour or that colour?" When dealing with appointments or bookings the question is "Would you like an appointment today or later in the week?"

What needs to be avoided are questions with a Yes/No answer like "Do you want an appointment?" or "Do you want to buy one of these designs?" As we have spoken about earlier, the trick here is to not give the opportunity to say no, but to make a choice between the two options offered. If the customer really doesn't know or doesn't want to make an appointment they will tell you. Consider that this process is doing them a favour by gently organising them for their next step so they don't have to think about it and have everything organised when they leave.

The other variation on this process to close a sale or appointment is to say "Would you like it to be soon, like today or tomorrow or would you like to wait a long time like next week?" At a psychological level, waiting a 'long time' may be appropriate for a bigger decision but you have set the time frame for completion and not left it open ended.

9 Find the person's "Key Motivating Factors"

Key Motivating Factors (KMFs) are the real reason they want to buy something. In the process of building rapport with the customer, your discussion will be around the product or service that you are offering, but in your discussion you need to find out why they are considering this product and what are the main benefits they are looking to receive from the product. The first reasons you will get may be physical or practical but you should delve deeper to find the emotional reason behind the desire for the product.

For example, why does a 50+ year old lady want to suddenly join a gym? In conversation, she mentioned her husband a few times, her health and not getting any younger and an off-hand comment about the new young fit woman who has started at her husband's office and seemed to have caught his eye. So, her KMF is to develop a fit and sexy body to keep her husband interested.

Once the KMF has been established, you can keep returning to it to close the deal or sell the product. "How impressed will your *husband* be with you, when he sees you have dropped 5 kg and looking fantastic so quickly – all because you made this purchase today?" It can also be used to keep her motivated while doing the exercise programs in the gym. So always focus on the issues that are important for the customer in front of you – information about how great the equipment is or the fact that you have child-care are completely irrelevant to that person.

Find the KMFs and the emotional reasons behind the interest for the product and use these tools to close the sale.

🔟 Customers love to be remembered

We have all had the experience of the local shopkeeper that has been in business in town for years, everyone knows him and he knows everyone. He is very friendly and always keen to chat. He surprises you because he remembers things about your last visit that even you had forgotten. Actually, he does not have the best business in town and may be a little slower than the competition. He may also not be the cheapest but his shop is where you are most comfortable taking your business. And interestingly, you probably recommend him to your friends! This is an example of great rapport and how it overcomes other negatives in a business. Imagine how well his business would flourish if he was actually really good at his work too!

This skill comes naturally for some people but it can be cultivated in any business or industry. When customers come to your business or when you speak to them on the phone, make a note of their name and what you casually spoke about the last time you met. This tactic is brilliant for corporations and large companies where trust and faith in your company by other corporates to for partnerships, investments or establishing contracts. It is also very important for executives that need to build trust and maintain large networks. It all comes down to building rapport with this as a key strategy.

Whatever you use for your appointments or meetings, make a point of jotting down the conversation you last spoke about. For example, it may be that the person's son was trying out for the football club, if he is married and the name of his wife, or where he said they were going on holiday or that surgery his family member was having. Anything that shows you paid attention and were listening attentively. This goes a long way in building strong positive rapport that will have your customers coming back and back for years to come.

The practical way of doing this is to add notes to each person's contact details in your phone or create an electronic file with customer information. Sales staff that visit multiple businesses regularly are skilled at this process but it is a good strategy even for regular businesses especially where contact with customers and clients occurs irregularly and the details of each person is difficult to remember over time.

11 Over-deliver – Give something extra as a pleasant surprise

Imagine being able to surprise your customers in some way with an extra little something, a bonus gift, an extra small service offered with their next visit or even extra thoughtfulness. Surprises don't even have to cost, simply taking the customer to the car, holding the door for them, going the extra mile, making that phone call to chase up that item extra for them, or giving them the contact details of someone who can help them.

Be that business that people talk about when the topic of going that extra mile is raised. Just when you thought the sale or service is complete, think what else can we do to impress with our great service by over-delivering. In years to come customers might not remember what they bought from you over the years or the price but they will remember the emotion of always being *surprised* with great service.

To reinforce how nice it feels, just think back to a time that you got a complimentary dish at a restaurant, free chocolates on your bed in the hotel, flowers or the extra service item added on the house. How nice did it feel? It reinforces that the business values the customer and does leave that warm and fuzzy feeling that is worth more than a price reduction. Think in your own business what extras can be added on or provided that creates this extra appreciation from the customer and differentiation from your competitors.

This eleventh item was the over-delivery for this chapter!

Summary

Practice your skills of rapport and these specific 11 strategies for providing excellence in customer service. They will boost your company's reputation compared to the competition, increase in sales and at the same time, you will enjoy the process enormously more.

Whatever business you are in, you are providing a service or a product that the customer wants and they will enjoy the benefits – so have fun, be happy and enjoy the process as the aim is for a win–win situation for everyone!

CHAPTER 8

Step 8 – Toolbox of Positive Techniques

CHAPTER 8

Step 8 – Toolbox of Positive Techniques

"How did you play the game of life today? Did you make any home runs or were you on the bench for the entire game?"

– Eli McIntosh

In this chapter, we are going to give you some extra tools and techniques that you can use that will improve your own skills and resilience, as well as extra processes to use when dealing with other people.

Attitude of Gratitude

This is a state of mind that you should be striving towards all the time. The impact is so profound that whole books have been written on this subject, and we are going to cover it for you in less than a chapter. This will give you the tools to use this powerful technique and it really does work!

The underlying principle is that we need to be grateful and recognise the wonderful things that happen to us every day. This reinforces the positive events in our lives and focuses our minds on what is wonderful and great even when we may be struggling with other life challenges.

This shifts your thinking and your emotions away from what is negative and draining, to what is good, uplifting and inspiring. The other challenges will still need to be addressed but you can set aside specific time to work on those issues. After that move your focus back to the wonderful things in your life.

If you dwell on the negative unresolved problems in your life most of the time, it will drag you down and you will not see the everyday wonders with which you are blessed. Focusing on the positives also activates the creativity in your mind that results in solutions that solve the problem.

We can always find something to complain about if we allow the negatives to be our focus, but this will just attract more of the same bad stuff over time. Finding and searching for the positives in a situation is the fundamental aspect of the "Attitude of Gratitude," and goes hand in hand with developing a positive mindset and environment.

Gratitude Exercise

Before going to sleep every night, think of three things that you can be thankful for or experiences that went well that day. Consider new skills that you have learned, generous or altruistic acts that you have done, or compliments that you have received from others. It is also important to enjoy the victories that you have had and when projects or difficult tasks are completed.

By thinking about three great things that happened each day, you reinforce your positive attitude and keep the great and wonderful things in front of you. This has a profound effect on your physiology, releasing the feel-good hormones and stimulating your amygdala. Those great thoughts should also give you better quality sleep and you are likely to have better dreams too!

Gratitude in the Workplace

Make a habit of thanking or congratulating three people at work every day for jobs well done or if they have been particularly helpful to you. This needs to be sincere and truthful and without any expectation of return. Make it brief and then continue on with your usual tasks so that the message is clearly that they are doing a great job, you recognise their achievements, appreciate it and expect nothing in return.

This process overcomes the common problem of workers only get feedback when they have done something wrong and there is no positive feedback for jobs done well. The unfortunate outcome with this is that they consider that they are no good at the job because they only get negative feedback.

Instituting this positive feedback by all staff to three others every day will result in improved self-belief, happier workers and increased resilience. The positive inputs for each worker gives them the understanding that they are doing well and their positive bank of compliments buffer them from the negative events when they do occur.

Get Everyone to Buy into Positivity Principles

Creating a positive workplace requires the commitment by all staff and workers. While the decision may start at the top or the bottom of the organisation, for it to be sustained and long term there has to be 'buy-in' from the owners or managers in charge. This is critical for success because if the senior staff are not leading by example and using positive processes in their dealings with staff and customers, the whole principle will be undermined.

In reality, it sometimes is the boss that is the 'problem' in the organisation and will take a brave employee to pull the boss up in their negativity or derogatory manners. At the end of the day, it is the bosses company so they will reap the rewards or losses and approaching it from the profit angle may allow the approach to be made. For example, make the suggestion that the organisation introduces the 'CEO Principles' processes and see how it goes. Give the boss this book to read and hopefully the benefits will be so clear that the decision will be the right one!

All other staff can be kept in line because of the established expectations of the business and the culture statements, so even if they don't like it, that is the business requirement. In reality, the staff that are habitually negative and can't operate without denigration, gossip, sarcasm and backbiting will probably leave and look for work elsewhere as it becomes intolerable for them to cope!

Use Positive and Supportive Language

Awareness of the words you and others in the workplace use is important as they set the tone of the workplace. The simplest example is when staff members are asked to do a particular job or extra task, the best responses are "I would love to", "Absolutely, I would be happy to help out" or "Anytime! You always help me so it's nice to return the favour!"

The negative language would involve comments like "That's not my job", "Is there no-one else that can do it?", "If I have to" etc. At the end of the day with the job still being done by that employee, which workplace is the happier and healthier one?

Language is also important in dealing with problems and mistakes. Avoid creating dramas and catastrophes and do not overstate the gravity of situations while realistically facing the actual problem. Problems can be termed 'difficulties' or 'challenges', mistakes can be termed as 'areas needing improvement' and crises can be 'high priority challenges'. Examples of positive and negative terms are listed below:

Negative	Positive
Problems	Challenges / difficulties
Mistakes/wrong	Area needing improvement
Crisis	Urgent challenge
Unskilled worker	Worker with incomplete training
Lazy worker	Worker lacking motivation/dedication
Boredom/boring	Need to find more interest
Terrible day	Not our best day/room for improvement
Bad	Room for improvement
Dumb/stupid	Needing assistance in some areas
Stubborn	Persistent

Of course, it is important that the problem (challenge) that you are facing is very clearly defined so you know exactly what you have to deal with. However, the severity of this problem does not need to be verbalised or explained outside of the business or to staff inside the business who do not need to know. Only share challenges with staff when they are in the position to fix it or if they need to know for some reason. This way your staff members are only dealing with relevant problems and not overloaded with problems that are outside their realm of responsibility.

Other keys to good communication are:

1. Keep it simple and avoid double meanings, double negatives, and innuendo.

2. Focus on the issue at hand and not any personal attitudes about the issue.

3. Make your view on the issue clear, and if there is something that you want or you want things to be done in a certain way, be clear so that the person knows exactly what you are talking about.

4. You may want to explain why things need to be done that way depending on the relationship with that person (partner, child, boss, junior), but the key is to be specific with instructions. For example, "Please make sure that the phones are answered in three rings" rather than "Please answer the phones quickly".

5. Focus on the positives in the situation. If a single problem has arisen in a process, don't focus only on the single problem but remind everyone how he or she is doing so well with all the other processes. Build them up emotionally before discussing the 'area where some improvement could be seen' or the area 'where things aren't going as smoothly as we would like'.

6. After discussing the problem, restate how well the other areas are running so the focus of the problem is balanced or sandwiched with positives on both sides. The natural tendency to only focus on the problem gives everyone the idea that 'everything is a catastrophe' or that 'we are all doing such a terrible job'. It is more often the case that the correction is a very small part of the whole system that overall is going very well, so make sure that this emphasis is conveyed in your discussions.

Consider Visual, Auditory and Kinaesthetic

When you have to discuss more complicated problems or issues relating to NITs from third parties, use the communication form that suits each of their personalities. You may like to refer to Chapter 2 and the descriptions of visual, auditory or kinaesthetic. Obviously you need pay attention to how the other person operates to work out their communication type. Only then can you use the terms and phrases that they will respond to and understand best. So in discussions use terms like "I see your problem", "I hear what you are saying" or "I understand how you must feel". These are useful for the visual, auditory and kinaesthetic people respectively, and they will understand much better if you keep the analogies along these lines.

Reinforce Positivity Everyday – signage, verbally and through computer programs

The Vision and Culture Statements of the business should be visible to the staff and customers every day on public signage or screens in waiting rooms or public areas and on all the commonly used stationery. When the primary message is a safety message, then the logo can be on the uniforms e.g. 'Safety First'.

Spreading the 'Attitude of Gratitude' around all the workers every day helps this process. The business can also reinforce the culture using pop-ups on each employee's computer with positive messages of welcome and goodbye at log on and log off. Regular pop-ups can also be programmed to occur giving the employee a 'Thought for the Day' and regular reminders of the Culture Statements one at a time. This system can also create a reminder for staff every hour to stand up and stretch every hour and give some guided exercises to ensure good muscle tone and blood flow is occurring. This is known to improve mental performance and reduce injuries both of which worsen with prolonged inactivity at the computer.

With the increasing prevalence of smartphone apps, these can also be programmed to message the staff with the positive thoughts for the day, Culture Statements and personal messages of appreciation from the company.

The process of prestart exercise programs for all staff is normal corporate expectation in Japan and China and only occasionally used in Western countries. The time can also be used to reinforce the culture and the work targets for the day. This process has a number of benefits from the physical benefits of improved fitness and reduced injuries to the improved mental processing and group motivation that occurs.

Potential to Prevent Suicide

Death rates from suicide in developed countries are around 10–12 per 100,000 people. This means that more people die from suicide than road accidents every year – 20% more in the USA, 90% more in Australia and 400% more in the UK! Suicide is the biggest killer of men under 44 and women under 35 in Australia, and it is preventable. Suicide rates are also four times higher for men than women. So this is a very common problem and everyone in the workplace can help to play a role and save a person's life!

Paying attention to statements that are being made by co-workers may identify those that are developing suicidal thoughts. A simple understanding of what these features are can allow you to recognise the tell-tale signs of deteriorating mood and you may be able to get them help and save their life.

As individuals become more depressed, their thoughts and comments become more negative and derogatory. These thoughts are often aimed at themselves, but they may also be aimed at anyone in work situations or their family. As the depressive thinking becomes more powerful, everything in the persons' lives becomes harder to do and less pleasurable. This often gets to the point where they stop performing hobbies, sports and don't even get pleasure from sex.

Their relationships with their partner or friends start breaking down and this is often used as the reason for them to be feeling down. However they may consider that they are feeling low because they are having the relationship trouble rather than their low mood and negativity causing the relationship breakdown. In the workplace, their relationships with co-workers and superiors also break down as they may become aggressive or abusive, or they may become reclusive and withdraw from social interactions.

It needs to be remembered that the two extremes are the verbally profuse person who has bad things to say about everything, and the person who just shrinks back into their shell and says nothing. Unfortunately, inside the passive exterior of this second picture may be a personal hell that their co-workers don't understand and may not feel able to cope with. However, as their co-worker, enormous help and support can be achieved with the simple sharing of concern for that person. Positive, open and non-judgmental support towards that person may be enough for that depressed person to verbalise their negative thoughts and therefore allow for professional help to be recommended and hopefully obtained.

Unfortunately, there have been many completed suicides where the introversion has never been questioned, and after the catastrophe, everyone feels terrible that "maybe something could have been done". Now is the time to start. Keep your eyes and ears open, recognise those NITs and where they appear to be invasive and overwhelming, encourage that person to seek professional support.

The good news for these people is that although depression is very common, with one in five people experiencing it at some stage in their lives, it can be successfully treated – often successfully improved in a matter of two to four weeks! The difference is like night and day for the sufferer, and the most common feedback that we get as health professionals from people after they have received treatment is that they wish that they had come for help sooner and not suffered the symptoms for so long. It is a very satisfying result to move people from that pit of despair and out into the light, joy and laughter that should be everyone's usual experience of life.

So, as the co-worker's "friend" you may:

- Ask questions about how they are going and how are they feeling.
- Mention that you have noticed that they are more irritable and 'cracking up' at the smallest things.
- Mention that their recent behaviour is unusual for them and they are difficult to be around.
- Just be open to offer your support or help.
- Quote lines from this book, if necessary, to allow the conversation to be started – or lend them the book!

The worst thing for these people is to be ignored and hope that it will just go away. Never be afraid to ask if they have had thoughts that life is not worth living, of harming themselves or committing suicide. If you can't speak about it, this reinforces the taboo, and when asked if they have had thoughts of death, the person will usually answer the question honestly, even if they underplay the intensity of the thoughts at first.

"A problem shared is a problem halved." Just allowing the person to vent will often help that person. Then some support and advice will make the person feel relieved and purged. Arm them with a few simple bits of information; you might point out that feelings of depression are very common, but you understand that treatment is very successful quite rapidly and that it can get you out of the black hole. Emphasise that they should see a doctor or professional to discuss it.

Passing on the information that they should not feel guilty or stupid is helpful. Depression is caused by a physical change in the brain that causes these feelings, and it can be corrected with treatment and just like high blood pressure, may need medication. There are also good quality websites giving detailed information about depression, how it occurs and how it can be successfully treated. Encourage them to see someone for professional treatment – it really works!

So, first pay attention, and then ask questions, offer support as a friend, let them know what you know about how successful the treatment is and if necessary advise on professional help. You may just save someone's life!

Of course, the other processes already described elsewhere that need to be practiced are:

- Don't react, respond
- Use mistakes as learning experiences
- Listen attentively and paraphrase to confirm
- Be a 'class act'
- Take 100% responsibility
- Use the Business Tree analogy

Summary

As a full-time worker, you will spend more awake time at work than anywhere else, so let's make workplaces wonderful environments for everyone! The steps to changing the work environment include:

- Educate your staff and co-workers.

- Develop an agreed workplace culture of a Positive environment.

- Deal with errors openly and without personal judgment.

- Look for system improvements to reduce errors.

- Recognise and support workers who show any possible depressive warning signs, and help to reduce the suicide rates.

A Positive Workplace creates rewards for the workers, clients and business owners as business profitability and reputation will outstrip your opponents.

Get started now!

CHAPTER 9

Step 9 – Positive Leadership Secrets

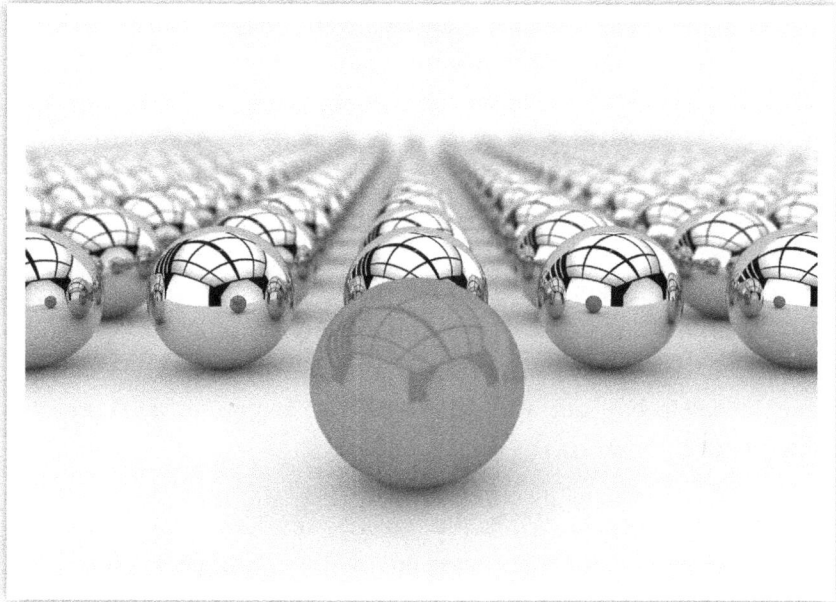

CHAPTER 9

Step 9 – Positive Leadership Secrets

"Any business is only as good as the people leading it, so choose your leaders well."

— Eli McIntosh

The creation of a spectacularly successful business is dependent on the leaders. You, the leaders, hold the key to the attitudes and success that flow through the business. Plant positive seeds with support and mutual benefit and everyone will blossom and take the business in an upwards spiral.

Walk the Talk

The leaders set the standards, the attitudes, the work ethic and the culture – and this is seen in what you do and how you do things, not just what you say. As the leaders, you hold the key and this positive approach needs to be from what you think, say and do, as this creates your character and destiny.

For success, you need to "Walk the Talk" – any lack of consistency will be very apparent in the business and it will be your actions that are copied and not your statements.

This change in attitude of leaders requires 100% commitment. Unless this commitment is present, do not waste your energy in paying lip service to a 'Positive Culture' if it is going to be undermined by the actions of the leaders.

The other serious aspect of leaders 'Walking the Talk' is that respect of your staff can be lost if there are double standards and it is clear that you are saying one thing and doing another. The double damage occurs because the business loses its positive atmosphere but as leader, you also lose all credibility and respect from everyone around.

The 3T's – Tasks, Timeframes and Targets

A common problem in larger organisations is failure to complete important tasks because urgent events keep taking priority. Typically the important tasks have less urgency but lead to improved productivity or profits but because there are pressing issues that the manager is faced with, those pressing issues get done and the important issues fall off their priority list.

The '3T's Strategy' solves this problem by providing a structured 'To Do' list that itemises all the actions that are needed by each manager including the task, the timeframe for its completion and the measurable target to record its completion.

This strategy changes the work environment from one where actions are planned but without the specific timeframes and targets being stated and jobs get put on the back burner and forgotten. Creating a 'To Do List' with the 3T's listed and stated for each staff member and manager results in more focus to complete the specific tasks and as thought has gone into the measure of success, the person is able to be clear about what they need to do.

This list of tasks should also be in a file that is accessible by up-line staff to allow all relevant managers to monitor how the task is progressing, which avoids the task being lost or delayed.

In areas of work where the manager has multiple tasks and everyday interruptions that pull them away from tasks at hand, it is very difficult to remember multiple tasks and where progress is at.

The list of each manager's or supervisor's 3T's list can be discussed at daily, weekly or monthly meetings and this keeps the momentum going and allows for easy reporting.

On completion of the task, the completed actions list should be archived and not deleted. This is because issues often recur and knowing what has occurred in the past and how matters were resolved is valuable especially if the person in the role changes.

A good example of that is when setting up a new facility or operation, all the actions required before that area can operate have been documented so that list can then be used when setting up the same process in the future.

Time Management Planner for Managers

In the same way that managers are often pulled away from important but not pressing issues, they can easily have their time used up inappropriately over the week in the same way as urgent demands are made on their time. This time management planner sets out the managers planned use of time to ensure that their important activities…

Look for 'Holes in the Bucket'

Most managers focus on building up workloads, increasing sales or marketing strategies. Just as important, and arguably more important than increasing turnover is the process of looking for the 'hole in the bucket' or where there are losses in the system.

The reason that 'holes in the bucket' are more important than increasing sales is that if you can find and fix holes that make savings of 10%, that will translate into 30% increase in profits if your profit margin is 30%. A 10% increase in turnover results in product or staff costs resulting in profits only increasing 3–7%, depending on your industry type. So, finding the 'holes in the bucket' has more impact than increasing sales!

Every staff member should be encouraged to look for inefficiencies in the systems that they are working with and find solutions. Encouraging and using the 'Brain Bank' of all your employees will result in many more innovative solutions to be brought forwards and savings should result.

Remember to publicly recognise and reward the staff that are creative and come up with solutions that are instituted. Using products from your own business is useful here as the cost to the business is wholesale but the employee enjoys the full value!

Be aware of Nonverbal Messages

To be an effective leader, you need to be aware of body language and nonverbal messages that you give out and that others are sending to you. It is amazing how strong these messages are and with only the roll of your eyes, you can show someone that an action was completely inappropriate or that you have no respect for that person or a third party.

A good example of this was when I received a complaint from a patient about the service that they received from a doctor was substandard. This was purely based on the fact that the next doctor they saw, simply rolled their eyes a single time after hearing the treatment plan but no words were spoken. The doctor that rolled their eyes had no idea of what they had done, the meaning that was taken by the patient or the flow on effects.

Leaders needs to be especially careful, create a poker face with empathy and concern but avoid the judgment step until you have the information from all sides.

Carefully watching other people's body language is also useful to be aware of how others are dealing with a situation, whether they are committed to a process and if they agree or disagree. Body language changes rapidly and unconsciously so individual issues can be recognised as being agreeable or disagreeable without words being spoken to the skilled body reader.

This is a wonderful skill to have if your role requires negotiated agreements, as you can be a step ahead of the others, until you come up against the skilled negotiators who have enough self-control to not react and are also able to reach you.

Build your Skill in Rapport

Building rapport skills is a very useful tool to learn when dealing with people in any situation. Clearly as a leader, you need to have the skills in communication and leading people but all good leaders create rapport. This allows you to lead the other person down the desired path without the person realising that they are being led down that path, as mutual benefits will are seen.

The process requires recognition of body language, verbal and physical cues from the eyes, skin, posture and mannerisms. There are techniques to create the other person's trust and belief with matching postures, creating empathy and the understanding that you are both on the same side, not against each other. Once rapport is established, it is amazing how supportive and compliant people will be, often giving you more than you wanted or asked for!

An example of this was in a restaurant where the main waitress was clearly stressed, overworked and understaffed, resulting in delays in taking orders and delivery of the food. We had the option of getting angry and complaining but instead Elizabeth congratulated her on "what a great job she was doing considering she was so understaffed". "I know how it feels," Elizabeth said, "because we have run restaurants and have been in exactly the same position ourselves…" etc.

Out came the full story from the waitress about how she was the only one there to cover the restaurant as other staff had called in sick and there was no support from management. All we did after that was to show our sympathy and support and a few more congratulations on how well she is coping and everything is getting done well. Her manner after that was visibly happier, smiling and less stressed. What Elizabeth recognised that she needed was to be recognised as doing a great job so in two sentences, developed rapport and it changed the girl's night.

As often happens, karma swings round and when we went up to pay, she gave us the desserts and coffee for free! Rapport created the trust from the waitress to accept the recognition and if the managers had been in, we would have hoped that they would have performed that duty – so stay aware of how your staff members are going, create the rapport and recognise them when warranted. Positive words are so powerful!

Teaching of rapport is a full seminar and is very valuable for all senior staff, managers and supervisors that are directly responsible for others. Sales staff are the other group where rapport is critical to success and undoubtedly, all the good sales staff will be achieving this through rapport building. Some do it naturally but training allows the specific processes to be recognised and refined.

Training workshops are available from a few hours to a few days but there are also online options to refine your skills in this area. Check our website for details on training packages for rapport in business.

Maintain a Class Act

The quality of an individual becomes most apparent when the chips are down and the situation is catastrophic. As a leader, you have to act calmly and professionally, working through the problem that has just created the 'catastrophe' and find solutions to the situation.

Losing your cool, becoming agitated, swearing and attributing blame does not help find the solution. Calmly ensure that everyone is focused in the right direction in the heat of the crisis and lead by example. After the crisis has settled and the heat is out of the event, you can then work through the steps of working out how the situation arose, where the source of the problem was and putting in place processes to avoid it happening again.

There is no excuse for bad behaviour at any time because that sends the message that it is acceptable to behave like that and suddenly years of hard work to create an encouraging, supportive and positive environment is lost.

Expect the Best

The Mission and Culture Statements have been set to expect high standards and this needs to be followed through with expectations at every level to be high, better than the competition and to lead the field. Using the terminology from your own cultures statements allows the message to be given out in a consistent, clear and positive manner.

Approaching this situation by asking questions to the employee is easier and less confrontational. You can ask them how they think that they are going, are there any aspects of their work that they think could be improved, or more directly "How would you rate your performance in the … job?" Or "Were there any areas that you think could have been improved?"

As in 'Walk the Talk', this applies to all aspects of your own behaviour performance as well as your behaviours and actions will be gold standard that the rest of the employees follow.

'No NITs' Days

'No NITs Days' can be run as events in workplaces where the day of awareness is promoted and advertised and everyone on staff follows the principles, wears badges and places signs up for the customers to be aware of the promotion. Any staff caught slipping out NITs puts money into a 'NITs box' and that money is used for a party or to add to the social fund for a later event.

The benefit of this is that the business is promoting itself as a positive workplace to the workers and customers and the 'No NITs' message is being reinforced to the workers. Plus the understanding is being spread to the customers and wider community, and the whole process should be fun and positive.

Guides and free downloads are available on our website for any business looking to run 'No NITs Days'. The message can be promoted strongly through traditional and social media to create maximum impact. Involve your local papers, TV and radio as they are always interested in positive stories and this one adds a degree of uniqueness resulting in the likelihood of getting free promotion of your business as well.

These 'No NITs Days' could be expanded to involve other organisations, towns or even the whole country! The more people that understand the principles, the better life will be for all of us.

When the possibility of a 'No NITs Day' arises for you, take advantage to reinforce the positive approach to life and culture around you and your business!

Workplace Barometer – tracking your business and your people

Mental health costs Australian businesses alone $10 billion and total costs of mental illness to the country is $33 billion. Mental health injuries are the fastest rising and most common WorkCover claim after musculoskeletal injury. We these figures being duplicated in around the world, action needs to be taken by employers for protection and early recognition of mental illness in the workplace.

Using validated questionnaires, the Workplace Barometer is a confidential employee questionnaire that measures all the important parameters in the workplace. This includes the workplace atmosphere, the effectiveness of the team, the positivity, resilience and mood of the workers including stress, anxiety and depression. This barometer therefore measures results at any one point to assess the workplace, the team and the workers within each team and can be repeated at regular intervals to watch for changes over time.

There are obvious benefits from the overall perspective of the atmosphere of the workplace and measure the effects of interventions or changes to staff or situations. The team function gives good indication on how people are working together and the assessments of individual worker's attitudes, resilience and mood will highlight the staff members at risk of stress related or depressive type issues.

The results are portrayed in a pictorial form, like a radar, for ease of interpretation and rapid recognition of the at-risk individuals. Interventions will see obvious changes to the shape with easy recognition of improvement or deterioration.

The huge benefit from performing the questionnaire regularly, such as three monthly, is that individuals that are struggling or deteriorating in their mood, will be identified. This early detection allows support or intervention to be put in to place to solve the issue before a crisis arises.

Compare this process to the traditional one where employees usually only get help after their crisis has occurred and they are unfit to work, have had an attempted suicide, or are significantly underperforming. Even though companies are willing to pay for Employee Assistance Programs (EAPs), the workers often do not access them until it is too late.

This process has the potential to identify the employees at risk of suicide using validated questionnaires that are reliable and reproducible. It is hoped and expected that using this monitoring and early intervention process, along with the Positivity Training in the Workplace will reduce mental health illness, sick leave, absenteeism and presenteeism as well as suicide.

In order for compliance and honesty to be obtained, the questionnaires are performed confidentially from the company with results de-identified and grouped together as averages. However any at-risk employees with scores indicating significant issues of mood disorder or coping difficulties would be contacted by the medical provider to discuss their results and offered intervention. This would all be private and confidential unless the employee requested disclosure to the company.

The other group that would be recognised is the 36% of the workforce that suffers from moderate to severe stress at work. Intervention and improved coping strategies can be targeted at this group to prevent them from becoming mental health illness statistics.

This exciting new service is available and addresses major problems of recognising the at-risk employees and has the potential to dramatically reduce mental health absenteeism and suicide rates. Every life saved is a success but many lives would be expected to be saved over time making this a very worthy cause!

Accreditation of Positive Workplaces

Certification from the International Positivity Institute for your workplace as an Accredited Positive Workplace is available. This creates more credibility for your business's commitment to creating and maintaining the positive culture to the staff and customers. It does set your workplace apart from others so should improve your ability to attract quality staff and this has been the case in several businesses that have adopted the Positive Culture.

By placing value on your greatest asset, your staff and being recognised officially for developing and maintaining this process, you are also likely to attract more customers who see value in that higher goal. The improved atmosphere and customer service that is achieved will improve customer loyalty and publicising those higher standards in your business and marketing gets the higher value message out as a point of difference to your competitors.

In markets that are very competitive, providing an Accredited Positive Workplace for staff wellbeing places you apart from the competition and will attract and hopefully retain quality staff.

Authentic Leadership

The term 'Authentic Leadership' made an entrance on the corporate world around 2003 and since then there has been a trend for managers, executives and leaders to step beyond the status quo and into this higher level of functioning.

The word authentic means not false or copied, genuine, real. When the term 'Authentic Leadership' is used, its meaning has expanded past the simple truth qualities and included higher functioning requirements like insight, sensitivity, integrity, taking initiative and working for the benefit of all in ethical ways. The other aspect of Authentic Leadership is that the focus is on positive outcomes for all concerned and not the focus on profits over everything else.

Given these higher-level qualities required of Authentic Leadership, this becomes a reflection of the person's character. If one's character is lacking in some areas, so will be the leader. It is therefore necessary to use insight to recognise any deficiencies and correct them or work around them.

Positive Mindfulness Cognition and the various techniques in this book that approach challenges in a positive manner, with respect and decency for all concerned and with the ethical expectation of working towards a win, win win outcome are all essential as you move towards achieving high functioning, Authentic Leadership.

Authentic Leadership does not require perfection but does require the features listed here.

Honest, genuine and diplomatic:
Firstly, authentic means real, truthful and not false. One who leads with openness and transparency and being free from deception or hidden agendas will win the confidence and trust of their staff. When a leader has the trust of their team, they are able to encourage all to follow their direction without resistance or double questioning, as they trust their leaders' decisions.

Honesty is a fantastic place to start, but there is so much more to be considered then just being honest. Honesty is about being in truth, but when you are in a position of leadership dealing with real people, honesty by itself is not enough. You must be able to exercise tact and diplomacy in all situations to produce a positive productive outcome or you will find your 'honesty' will very quickly personally insult and upset your team leading to resistance, resentment and dwindling admiration.

Ethical:

A leader exhibiting this quality quickly gains respect and admiration from their team and associates. They are known to consider all angles keeping focused on doing what is right, fair and just, regarding individuals, business and even the environment.

Ethical leaders should show this characteristic in their personal and business lives. Clearly lack of consistency in these qualities implies falsehood, and so undermines their authenticity. Usually quality leaders have gained strength of character through life's experiences and are able to draw positively on these valuable lessons when leading a team and show the traits of ethical behaviour when managing difficult situations. Having and ethical approach to all situations reflects a higher degree of wisdom with awareness for the higher qualities of life. Displaying ethical behaviour is therefore a highly-valued characteristic in any individual in business.

Positive attitude:

One cannot expect to lead other people with purpose without a positive 'can-do' attitude. This is particularly important in times where adversity strikes or there is the need to motivate a team to succeed against the odds. The ability to keep a team focused on a positive plan of action and never give up will see the project completed with this positive determined mindset that is wonderfully contagious. It is also true that a positive leader encourages and gently stretches others, and gives them confidence to strive for higher goals, getting the very best out of their team.

The opposite way of leading is by fear, this type of leadership tends to not be sustainable as staff do not want to be exposed to that level of anxiety every day. The threat of bad consequences drags the team down and the team is not able to operate from a place of high motivation. Employees will feel unsatisfied, unvalued, are only looking forwards to the end of the day and are likely to look for work elsewhere.

Insightful – 'beyond vision':

A leader with vision is often featured as a key feature of Authentic Leadership, but a more important trait is to have insight. Insight is said to be beyond vision, the ability to see deeper than what is presented on the surface, to be able to delve into the depths of a situation and uncover the whole picture from all angles, leaving no stone unturned.

Leaders with insight will not be classed as impetuous or impulsive, but spend time contemplating the situation, realising that some things aren't always what first appears. A leader exhibiting insightfulness holds the vision clearly always and is patient waiting for all things to be presented, bringing forth a more accurate meaning to the phrase 'all things considered'.

Deep sense of purpose:

The most successful businesses are driven by passion which comes from the deep sense of purpose. This deep sense of purpose is easy to sell to have the team buy into to your goals. It is more than just working towards set goals because the deep purpose draws on a spring of inner passion and motivates themselves and the whole team to performance above expectation to achieve the great outcomes.

Focused on building success:

An Authentic Leader focuses on success, not only for their own business but for in the personal lives of all their employees and the other businesses they deal with. This is the way that long term success is fostered as all parties are gaining from the relationship so all will work together on an ongoing basis.

Within the business, the leader has to be focused on the growth and success of the business, treating it as if it were their own. They constantly monitoring the level of performance and financial success and they are always looking for improvements in efficiency and reducing waste. The good leaders have their eye on the ball at all times.

As stated in the 'Tree Analogy', the health and wellness of the business must come first because this is what sustains everyone else's wages so must thrive.

Demonstrates self-discipline:
Self-discipline is a much-needed skill and needs to be displayed as a great leader. This comes in many forms from personal lifestyle choices (like exercise, diet and alcohol) to managing stress, dealing with difficult situations and controlling your emotions and reactions.

As a leader, the stresses and workload can be high, and it is crucial to think on your feet and make important decisions fast with 'all things considered'. If leaders don't keep these stresses under control and show a calm and even temperament, the staff will lose respect and confidence in their leading ability.

We have talked in our previous chapters about "Responding, Not Reacting", leading with "Intelligence, Not Emotion" and remembering that the only place for drama is on the stage. It is almost impossible to be able to think with clarity using the intellect to arrive at the best conclusion if one is consumed by emotion – one would then make a call based on a clouded mind.

Leading with Heart:
Compassion is not to be confused with weakness. A leader that shows heart will win the respect of their subordinates. As long as the business in not compromised and all clearly understand it must take precedence, flexibility and individual's personal situations should be considered on some level. We have talked about the partnership between employee and employer as relationship, like any other a 'give and take' needs to be balance for sustainability long term. A leader that displays compassion will find their team will be willing to extend themselves without drama or feeling they are being abused when asked to do more shifts. The moment the relationship tips the scales too much on one side it should be quickly balanced so neither party ever feels like they are taken for granted.

'Positive Mindfulness Cognition' Training

Positive Mindfulness Cognition (PMC) training is the process of making individuals aware of their own thoughts, teaching strategies to control these thoughts to create a positive mindset. Across whole workplaces this is very powerful, resulting in benefits across the board. Adding in the other processes of rapport, resilience, positive approach, motivation, goal-setting, self-worth, gratitude and honouring others adds power and magnifies the benefits for the businesses and individuals alike.

All of these processes lead to dynamic, mindful, authentic leaders and motivated, results focused staff and epic human beings!

Summary

Organisations are dependent on their leaders to set the standards and consistently take the actions that they expect to be performed throughout the organisations. Failure to do so is like a cancer that will spread through the organisation and sets up precedents of double standards and hypocrisy.

Leaders need to develop their skills in:

- use and recognition of body language

- building rapport

- setting work goals with the 3T's
  (Tasks, Timeframes and Targets)

- Fixing the holes in the bucket

- Running 'No NITs' days

- Accrediting the business as a 'Positive Workplace'

- Work towards Authentic Leadership

Lastly, use the Workplace Barometer regularly to monitor your business atmosphere, the effectiveness of your teams and your staff's mental health levels. This unique program uses validated assessments for early detection of problems in individuals and will allow early intervention in your business to save the business money and could save lives from suicide!

CHAPTER 10

Four Steps to Achieving a Positive Bottom Line

CHAPTER 10

Four Steps to Achieving a Positive Bottom Line

"Failing to plan means that you plan to fail."

– Unknown

At the end of the day, week or year, it is the financial bottom line that is the most fundamental criterion that needs to be positive. However great everything else is, the business cannot be sustainable unless the financials are sound. It is a sad fact that many people running businesses are not trained in finances and this is revealed by the fact that 95% of businesses close in the first few years of operation.

Many university and colleges courses produce skilled professionals and workers in every field, usually without a single lecture on business management and financial requirements. In this chapter, we are going to cover some of the key financial parameters that will allow better forward planning and financial management to achieve success.

Of course, all the information given here is general in nature and independent financial advice needs to be obtained for everyone's specific situation. This will be great starting point for new business operators and a review for the others.

Step 1 Set up a Cash Flow Budget in Advance

Cash is king and the most common reason for businesses to fail in the early days is delays in cash flow. As you are planning to start your new business, you need to have detailed cash flow budgets with realistic figures of all your incomes and expenditures.

Understanding the timing of how your income will come in is critical because some companies will only pay 30 days after receipt of an account and only at the end of that month. Therefore from the outset, you may need to be hard-nosed and require other businesses to pay you within 7 or 14 days of the account, even though that is harder when you are trying to get the business.

You also have to allow for bad debtors and the delay in the build-up of sales in your budgeting. In the early stages, it is much better to be very conservative for your sales figures and overstate your expenses so you have a buffer in place, rather than be optimistic an suffer the cash flow shortfall resulting in the inability to pay your essential bills like staff wages, rent or electricity!

Most outgoings can be predicted reasonably well like rent, electricity, council fees, wages, advertising and cost of goods. Some businesses such as hospitality have waste that is hard to predict and needs to be monitored from the outset, as this alone can the difference between success and failure. If income is not good enough, an increased amount for advertising may be needed to boost sales so variables can occur here quite commonly.

Income levels are probably the hardest to judge in advance. Whatever your best guess is, you need to watch the actuals compared to the estimates in the first few weeks and months of the business, along with your expenses. This will allow you to modify your budgets to match reality so that you know exactly where you are heading – to success or down the gurgler! Failure to pay attention is suicide…

In the first few months of your business, these need to be reviewed weekly and then fortnightly, only reducing to monthly when you are confident that your figures are above breakeven and your forward planning shows financial security. It does not need to take a long time and a simple spread sheet with extrapolated figures is all that you need to create. Ask your accountant or skilled bookkeeper to create them for you if you don't have those skills yourself.

You can then use these monthly budget figures in the long term. As the expenses and incomes become more clear, put in your planned changes or growth expectations and see how the figures change. They need to be set for at least a year ahead, and preferably run them three years ahead. When the business is reasonably stable, review them either monthly or quarterly – less frequent than this will result in too much time passing before you take action so business profitability is lost.

Step ❷ Work Out your Breakeven Point

The single most important figure you should know about your business is where your daily breakeven point is. Do you know yours? It is staggering how few business operators know this figure!

How much in come do you need to make to break-even – this is where you have not made any money but you have just covered all your expenses. You can look at your breakeven point as income on sales per day, number of services provided if you are in a service industry or number of hours that were chargeable if hourly rates are charged. You can create the most useful format that this figure takes to suit your business to make it easy to assess or communicate with staff. The dollar value of sales per day is the most obvious one but if you are in a service industry your targets may be 'X number' of clients or charge 'X hours' of fees per day.

Having this figure calculated and explained to staff gives everyone a clear target to aim for every day and can be used positively to watch the growth of the business over the weeks and months.

If this figure is not being reached regularly, then strong action needs to be taken as this is the alarm bells telling you that your business is not viable.

The way to work out your breakeven point is to take all your fixed overheads for a month and divide by the number of working days (20 or 22 if you work Monday to Fridays). You then need to work out your margins on goods sold and work out how many goods you need to sell to recover that amount of overhead. If you have staff working for a percentage, you use the same calculation but it is the percentage that you keep that is the figure you use to cover the overheads.

For example, if your fixed overheads are $10,000 per month at 20 working days that means your costs are $500/working day. If your product sells for $100 and your "profit" on that is 40% you get $40/product so your breakeven is $10,000 divided by $40 = 25. Therefore you need to sell 25 items (products or services) per day to breakeven.

It is absolutely critical that you know your daily, weekly and monthly breakeven points and that you watch your actual figures and match them against breakeven on a very regular basis.

Step ❸ Watch your Monthly KPIs (Key Performance Indicators)

Key Performance Indicators are a more detailed look into your monthly financials and give you the clues to show you how your business is going and to tease out where improvements can be made. While the breakeven point is a coarse figure that ensures survival, KPIs allow you to look critically at the different areas of your business and see where you have the ability to create better profits.

Every industry has KPIs that are available so that you can compare your business and expenses against others. Accountants will often have access to these and they are also available from lead industry bodies. There are some limitations with using other people's figures as their operational structure may be different and they may be basing their figures on different setups.

However, once you have been operating your own business and growth occurs, you can use your own KPIs to watch your own expenses in different areas to ensure that as you expand, you do not overspend in an area like management or in overall staff numbers compared to sales or services.

The production of KPIs is relatively simple if you are already tracking your monthly income and expenses and the standard financial software programs allow transfer of the monthly figures into a KPI spreadsheet. The detail within the KPIs that each business produces is their decision but it is critical to separate costs and income sources to reflect how the income and the expense for each product source. Other details like number of hours staff members work, number of sales or numbers clients seen need to be added in separately as they are not usually part of the financial software.

By then using simple arithmetic, you can generate figures like:

- Total income per month
- Total expenses per month
- Profit margin per month
- Total sales per sales person or provider
- Total income generated per sales person or provider
- Income generated per hour per provider (a more useful comparison)
- Average price per sale
- Average income generated per customer (
- Staff cost per sale
- Non-staff cost per sale
- Total cost per sale
- Staff hours per sale
- % services given reduced fees (eg discounts, special offers or bulk billing if medical)

Collecting these figures gives businesses some very useful information. Of course the most basic information is business profitability but it also allows you to see the profit margin per service that will allow you to more accurately adjust your breakeven point.

Individual performance figures can be compared to the average, so each person can see how the rank compare to others. This encourages them to pick up their performance if necessary and also gives them a good indication of money they are generating per hour. They will then often modify their actions to get their figures better for the next month and on an ongoing basis.

Some sales personnel or providers have a tendency to give reduced fees too easily and this is easily shown in these figures too. It is often the case that the ones that have high levels of reduced fees also have reduced total incomes and reduced hourly rates. These individuals can then be coached on the processes to close sales without compromising the fees being charged.

Number of 'staff hours per sale' is a really important one as it allows us to accurately judge if our staffing levels are good or excessive. We know that if our medical business is running effectively, our staff time per service is 20 minutes and when that figure grows to 30 minutes or more, we know that we do not need more staff but need to look at where the time is being wasted! This overcomes the 'we are so busy we need to employ more staff' claim that seems to be very common.

At a more detailed level, the KPIs can also monitor the levels of other costs like accounting, administration, legal, insurance and other smaller proportions that may change over time. If one area becomes out of proportion, the KPIs allow you to recognise this change and bring the excess costs back into line. Obviously this results in better bottom line for the business in the long term.

These KPIs are also very powerful tools to use when economic times become tight. They can be used to find areas of improvement and pick up fine details of increases in costs or falling incomes in specific areas. Knowing how you have been running over the long term allows in-depth assessment and this ability is likely to keep your head above water when your competitors are going under!

If your business operates from several separate sites or distinct departments, the figures in each area can be compared, and again this is information is gold. Disparities across areas and departments become very easy to detect and then investigation will show what the one is doing better or why the other area is underperforming, so can be fixed.

Many business operators fail to understand how small differences can make a huge difference to the bottom line. The famous economic example is that if you can reduce your expenses by 5% and increase your sales by 5%, your profits will probably rise by 30%. This is because if your profit margin is 30% and you increase profit by 10%, it rises by 30%. If your profit margin is only 10%, increasing it by 10% doubles your profit! Perhaps that will make you more interested to study your KPIs very carefully...

Many business operators don't bother monitoring these figures, even when they are explained or are even shown the figures for their own business. It is essential for KPIs to be created, studied and used to fine tune your business – they are your keys to business success. Just ask Warren Buffet – he knows all the answers are there in the numbers!

Step ④ Plan Ahead – legal, tax, investment and insurance advice

This last point is one of the aspects of business that most people do not like. It is the relatively boring, costly and painful process of protecting your business for the long term. While the acts all cost money and sometimes individuals choose to cut corners and avoid those costs, the long-term costs can be – and often are – devastating.

So this is all about forward planning for risks, tax liabilities, legal risks and insurance needs. All involve discussion with professionals and these professionals are going to advise you to pay out more money and protect your business and yourself in various ways. You have the choice to take each step or not, but the costs if any of those risks occur will be so costly that you will wish that you had listened.

Any business structure needs to have the correct legal structure, and any business with more than one owner needs to have a 'proper' partnership agreement with all the details of percentage share, internal control processes, dissolution processes, issues of intellectual property and many other legalities. Failure to set out the business ownership structure leads to conflict and lack of clarity, especially if the business becomes successful and you risk losing all your profits on the legal expenses of the settlement dispute.

Legal or accounting advisors will also give you advice on the actual legal structure that will best suit you to set up the business. There are multiple different structures that can be used in different countries, and they are called different names, but commonly individuals can operate a business in their own name, as a sole trader, in a company of various types, as a trust or even as a charity. There are different financial outcomes for income distribution, immediate tax, long-term capital gains tax and transfer implications, so this is a very important step to take and appreciate the good advice as it protects your future.

The structure can also create methods for distributing income to other individuals, partners, family members or other entities to reduce the taxable income. There are also tax benefits in holding or distributing the income in certain entities to stay in the lower tax brackets, for example superannuation funds and family trusts.

Accountants are very valuable to your business and should be used regularly and wisely. You can limit your accountancy fees by keeping good quality books and giving them complete and detailed records which reduces their workload. Submitting your annual returns is the mundane end of the accountant's value to you – their true value is for them to cast their professional eye over your figures and advise you if they can see any disparities compared to what they expect. Because they see multiple businesses of your type, they can probably give you advice on areas where you are out of line and where you should be tightening up your finances.

Accountants can also assist you with creating future budgets and helping you create your Budgets versus Actual figures, if you struggle with that. They will help in forward planning for tax liabilities and providing financial solutions to assist you – perhaps it is to reduce your tax, give you strategies to save for expected tax payments, superannuation and retirement strategies.

Another important area to ensure your business protection is in the insurance area. Every business needs insurance to cover for a wide range of risks. The most obvious is to protect the business assets with property, building, and contents insurance. All vehicles and assets that are mobile need to have specific cover with the insurer informed of the items in advance, especially if they are of high individual value.

Insurance is available to cover for loss of operation due to major events, and income protection insurance is available for individuals and businesses that provide income under specific conditions. Read those conditions carefully because if your loss of operation occurs for other reasons, there will be no pay out.

Individuals operating in your business with specific skills or professional risks need to have their professional indemnity up to date at all time.

While it is usual for professionals to pay for their own cover, the business needs to have the systems in place to ensure that this indemnity is up to date and paid every year.

The other risks within the business need to be assessed and ensure that appropriate cover is in place to cover any rare but expense failure. Cover for non-professional staff working with professionals may be required for the business in case the administrative staff fail to respond or communicate appropriately. This umbrella cover is often forgotten, but the professional indemnity will only kick in when the professional has made an error and is not responsible if the urgent message does not get to them.

Directors and officers' insurance is required when the organisation is run by a board and covers litigation against them as the responsible individuals for the organisation. Appropriate and professional standards are still required and the insurance does not protect if any breaches of law or company requirements occurs.

As organisations grow, it is useful to deal with a single insurance agent or organisation that has access to all the insurance companies and can advise on the best solutions for your business. This will save huge amounts of time to get their advice on the best solutions and what the benefits and risks are between the different options. Trying to compare 10–20 page insurance documents to work out what is missing in each one is extremely difficult as focusing on price alone will often leave you without appropriate cover.

The other advantages of having a dedicated agent is that it gives you a single point of contact when any claim is made and the joint policies that you bring to the table should allow better rates to be achieved, due to the volume provided. Obviously they need to be honest and trustworthy and not just trying to sell insurance that you don't need and not selling insurance from a particular company because their returns are greater.

While it may feel painful to pay out the money to have insurance, decide on how far you will go and what risks you are prepared to take. Make sure that you know the fine print and what risks are not covered and if possible, take your own practical precautions to avoid those events.

Lawyers, accountant and insurances all cost significant money but setting things up properly at the start and using them efficiently through your business growth is essential to protect and grow your business in the long term. Trying to avoid these costs will result in higher and potentially catastrophic costs in the future.

Summary

A positive financial bottom line is the aim of every business and the four essential steps to achieve this are:

Step 1   Create a Cash Flow Budget and work to that.

Step 2   Calculate your Breakeven Point. Ensure that every day you are operating above this level.

Step 3   Monitor your Monthly Key Performance Indicators. These allow you to refine performance and improve profitability.

Step 4   Plan ahead – get legal, accounting and insurance advice early and review regularly.

How World Leaders used Positivity for Phenomenal Success

CHAPTER 11

How World Leaders used Positivity for Phenomenal Success

"The brave may not live forever – but the cautious do not live at all"

– Richard Branson

The most successful businesses in history have used 'CEO Principles' to achieve success and catapult their companies so far above their competition that they stand alone. The principles are always the same – base the business philosophy on positivity at every level, ensure that all parties benefit, ensure that the aims of the business are inspirational and will improve society in some way that is greater than the service provided. The results speak for themselves with the leaders that work in this way head the world's richest people and are the individuals that own the leading companies in the world.

Bill Gates with Microsoft, Richard Branson with Virgin and Warren Buffet with Berkshire Hathaway immediately come to mind as the richest and most positive individuals in business. Over history, the most successful businesses in past used these principles too – Walt Disney always created positive messages in his productions and had positive self-belief with always doing what is best. Oprah Winfrey proves that where you come from does not dictate your future as long as you maintain a positive approach to life.

Any business leader can choose to use these principles in exactly the same way as these leaders and obtain the same exponential benefits. Therefore we will look into some of the world's most successful businesses to learn how they use these principles and the phenomenal outcomes that are achieved as a result.

Bill Gates and Microsoft

The world's richest person, Bill Gates, started in the garage with a dream in 1975 of having "a computer on every desk in every home" even though he had no idea how that could be achieved at that time. He understood that success required Microsoft to change the status quo and create better solutions for the whole world in how everything is done. Forty years later, Microsoft is behind almost every business, production line, communication and in every one of our personal lives without us even realising it!

Bill Gates also realised that success required the ability to "collaborate and share ideas with other people, and to sit down and talk with customers and get their feedback and understand their needs." He knew that he needed to get the best people in IT working with him to create these innovative new processes and needed to listen to what the consumers needed and wanted. Microsoft can confidently stand proud knowing that their programs have fundamentally changed communication, society, business operations and everyday life in positive ways. Positivity Principles are feature strongly across Bill Gates's operations. He states that "As we look forward into the next century, leaders will be those who empower others" and he confirms the view that "your most unhappy customers are your greatest source of learning".

This outward looking approach, where you are always trying to make sure that you are providing value to your customers and positive changes to their lives while at the same time producing social improvement has been the key to his business success. "Innovation is the real driver of progress" underpins his whole organisation, and employees of Microsoft are excited to know that they are also part of that process, and also responsible for changing the world into a better place.

Like all successful people, he has had negative experiences and failures and he emphasises the importance of the positive learning experience in these situations. "It is fine to celebrate your success but it is more important to heed the lessons of failure". He also understands the rapidity of change saying that "Intellectual property has the shelf life of a banana!"

Along with his phenomenal success, he commits to a world-changing vision in social justice. His lofty aspirations here are just as highflying as his Microsoft dream under the Bill and Melinda Gates Foundation. The aims here are to eradicate HIV/AIDS from the planet with the development of an effective vaccine, to create a pathway out of poverty by providing education and healthcare to the poorest communities and striving to eliminate discrimination. There is a strong focus on empowering the poorest people, especially women and girls, to transform their lives including family planning. Addressing nutrition issues, providing financial tools to the poor for self-improvement, teaching farmers to increase production sustainability, and college education completion are all examples of the difficult issues being addressed by the Foundation.

While being the richest man in the world, his world-changing vision is benefiting every single one of us in some way every day. Positivity Principles underpin all this success.

Warren Buffet – Berkshire Hathaway

As the third richest man in 2016 as ranked by Forbes, Warren Buffet is the world leader in financial Positivity! He defies the doomsayers, and bucks economic trends by continuing to grow his empire through the worst economic times. Amid stock market crashes, Global Financial Crises, banks imploding and currencies teetering on failure, he is the one figure that stands tall amongst the wreckage of the financial system! His undeniable optimism is seen in his active investment approach through the Global Financial Crisis and shown in his 2016 annual report when he stated that the "negative drumbeat" about the nation's prospects by the presidential candidates is "dead wrong".

On the other side, he is balanced and has insight to predict the risk of the investments that everyone else was keenly backing. Long Term Capital Management (LTCM) was the largest hedge fund start-up in history when it was launched in 1994 and Warren assessed this and decided that it was "too risky". The first three years showed amazing profits but, in 1998, Russia was unable to cover its debt and defaulted, creating panic selling and a global margin call. LTCM failed and had to be bailed out by the Federal Reserve. Warren Buffet was correct!

"The best defence in a tough economy is to add the most you can to society" he says, reinforcing the message about the importance of the bigger picture. Not only that but he reinforces the importance of the win–win principle stating "Help others and the fruit will be there. Wealth is worthless if you've destroyed all your relationships to attain it".

Berkshire Hathaway is a prime example of how Buffet has used Positivity Principles in business to create a hugely successful empire. He used the win–win philosophy to create a multifaceted business working with others to provide mutually beneficial results. He partnered with many different people with different skills and by joining forces both parties benefit equally, creating long-term, committed and stable businesses. Happy, profitable partners continue to work in the company to create growth and profits for everyone.

His advice is also to "Do what you are passionate about. If you do this, there will be few people competing or running faster than you." His view is that if you live with passion, life becomes a lot more fun and you are motivated to jump out of bed every day.

On positive thinking, Warren confirms the importance of gratitude when times are tough or you suffer backwards steps. "If you go from the first floor to the 100th floor of a building and then go back to the 98th, you feel worse than if you'd just gone from the first to the second, you know. But you've got fight that feeling because you are still on the 98th floor."

Warren also has a great technique for negative and unpleasant memories. He never dwells on anything unpleasant and views his memory like a bathtub. He only keeps memories and information in his bathtub that are useful and pleasant and all the other thoughts just gets drained through the plughole! First to go are the painful memories, followed by anything that may detract him from his goal of success. The medical research confirms that elimination of negative thoughts has major health benefits and you live longer!

He also openly admits being very influenced by Dale Carnegie's book *How To Win Friends and Influence People* and he was riveted by the first rule that states: "Don't criticise, condemn or complain." As he hated criticism himself, he incorporated these principles into his life with teaching and showing people better ways to perform rather than fall into the negativity of criticism.

The Positive philosophy extends to how he treats customers, staff and business partners. He knows that wealth is useless if you have destroyed your friends and relationships to achieve it. "We celebrate wealth only when it is fairly won and wisely used. Don't rush in a get greedy. Take the high road. It's far less crowded!"

This community-minded approach matched his $60bn contribution to the Gates Foundation – "because Bill Gates is the only person that would know how to use that sort of money," Warren Buffet said.

He also reinforces that failure is a learning experience, saying "You need to get your feet wet and some failure under your belt" and "If you are not failing, you are not learning."

Some of his other quotes are:

"We get worried when people start to agree with us!"

"Go to bed a little wiser than when you woke up" and "Learn something every day."

Warren Buffet shows how you can be quiet and self-contained and still create one of the largest and most successful businesses in the world. Positivity Principles again underpin this phenomenal success.

Richard Branson – Virgin

Richard Branson's meteoric rise to fame and fortune was based on boundless optimism, passion and fun! "More than anything, fun is the secret of Virgin's success!" He went against every business convention of the past, showing that creativity and positivity in the workplace can catapult success and motivate performance. He has made the point that he has never "gone into business purely to make money… It has to be fun and it has to exercise your creative instincts".

The focus on the business creating benefits for the greater good is highlighted when he said, "There is no greater thing you can do with your life and your work than follow your passions – in a way that serves the world and you". The importance of living your passion was reiterated with "Throwing yourself into a job you enjoy is of life's greatest pleasures". And you always see a smile on his face!

Never would personal limitations like his dyslexia, poor school performance or negative views from others, halt his optimistic approach to business and life. Solutions or ways around obstructions to his path were always found. Using the skills of others was critical to his success, proving that you do not have to have all the skills yourself to be successful.

He equally believes in not limiting your vision and aiming for the stars. His Virgin Galactica aims to be the first commercial space travel business and that brave step has significant challenges. "It is only by being bold that you will get anywhere. If you are a risk-taker, then the art is to protect the downside."

Positive Principles flow through the organisation, based on his philosophy that "Respect is how you treat everyone, not just those you want to impress". Going several steps further, he states "Train people well enough that they can leave, treat them well enough that they do not want to!" Creating a positive work environment gives dramatic results to the quality of service that customers receive and the level of job satisfaction of the employees. It is possible to "feel" or "sense" the positive atmosphere in a variety of Virgin businesses and this shows that even in huge organisations, the positive culture can penetrate through any international business.

Not only does he set Positive Principles in his business, in the early 1990s he shared all the proceeds of a British Airways compensation payout with the all the Virgin staff – the so called "BA bonus"!

Failures are treated by Branson as positives to learn from – "Don't be embarrassed by your failures, learn from them and start again". Also he uses the analogy that "You don't learn to walk by following rules. You learn to walk by doing and falling over". He also has the humility to say "Only a fool never changes his mind". When talking about leadership he says "Courage is what it takes to stand up and speak; courage is also what it takes to sit down and listen."

However, he not only puts his money behind his opinions but he put his life on the line too while attempting incredible goals. He has broken world records as the fastest Atlantic crossing in a yacht in 1986 after a previous attempt failed with capsizing and he needed to be rescued – still with a smile on his face! He broke the world balloon speed record in 1991, travelling at 245 mph (394kph) and made several attempts at balloon circumnavigations and while breaking records on the way. He broke the record for the fastest trip from Dover to Calais in an amphibious vehicle and in 2008 tried to break the Eastbound Atlantic crossing record in a 30m yacht with his children. Gale force winds and 12-metre seas battered and damaged the boat but they made it home safely.

Like other world leaders, he uses his passion to overcome major humanitarian issues, setting up "The Elders" with Peter Gabriel and Nelson Mandela formally commencing in 2007. This group aims to achieve peaceful solutions to longstanding conflicts and global issues that are causing human suffering. He is also the founding sponsor of the International Centre for Missing and Exploited Children (1999), the Carbon War Room (2009) to address global warming, Virgin Startup with 100 entrepreneurial loans in the UK and in South Africa with the Branson School of Entrepreneurship. He continues to be active in supporting the fight against global warming, in promoting universal access to broadband, the elimination of nuclear weapons (with Global Zero), wildlife protection and equality – he boycotted Uganda because of their anti-homosexuality laws stating that "people should be able to love whoever they want". He was listed as the No. 1 LGBT ally by the OUTstanding organisation in 2014.

Branson was knighted in 2000 to become "Sir Richard" because of his services to entrepreneurship, he was considered the most admired business person by the *Sunday Times* in 2014 and the No. 1 most influential British entrepreneur in 2015. There are multiple other awards to his name reflecting his commitment to a better world.

Other quotes:

"To be successful, you have to be out there, you have to hit the ground running."

"All you have in life is your reputation: if you lose your good name you'll never be happy."

Richard Branson was like a breath of fresh air to the business environment, showing that it is possible to create a hugely successful businesses that operates with fun, creativity, interpersonal respect and for the greater good – proving that Positivity Principles work in real life.

Walt Disney – Disney

Walt Disney created a huge industry based on positivity and spreading a positive message within the entertainment industry. Generations of all ages continue to be enthralled, are motivated and absorb positive principles through the films that were created and then inspired by Walt Disney.

Walt Disney suffered the hardships of the 1920s, with initial business failure and ongoing tough times and financial ruin in Missouri. His eternal optimism was shown when he sold his last camera to buy a one-way first-class ticket to Hollywood so that he would arrive in style in 1923. His studio suffered from mistreatment by the larger studios and distributors who owned the rights to all the productions. When faced with an ultimatum and worsening returns, he broke free to work independently, despite losing all his staff except one cartoonist to the bigger players, and started again in 1928. On three of four times in his life, he put his whole financial empire on the line to create the productions that he believed in and used his enthusiasm and optimism in himself and the vision to pull through the hard times.

The creation of Mickey Mouse at this time was the start of his business success and the early cartoons were comical and uplifting. Messages of right and wrong were progressively added to the films, creating learning experiences as well as entertainment. Walt Disney also bucked the status quo with his plan for a full-length animated feature film of *Snow White and the Seven Dwarves* being considered impossible – 'bound to fail' and 'will lead to bankruptcy' was the assessment of most people. With full colour and sound, it cost three times the budget at $1.5 million, but after release grossed $6.5 million by 1939, becoming the world's most successful movie at that time! Like Warren Buffet was to say later "If most people agree with the project, we are in trouble!" The list of subsequent and innovative films just kept on being produced such as *Dumbo, Fantasia, Sleeping Beauty, Mary Poppins* and many others.

Walt Disney is recognised as having the most fertile and unique imaginations in the world and along with his innovative processes in the film industry was able to take his dreams and vision into reality. His love of animals and history combined to create motion pictures that are considered to be 'modern art' and are now timeless testaments to his positivity.

Disney's big vision of a unique theme park came true in 1955 with the start of the Disneyland Parks. The $17 million investment soon multiplied tenfold and the theme parks spread to becoming a worldwide phenomenon.

The positive beliefs of Walt Disney are expressed in his quotes like:

"All our dreams can come true, if we have the courage to pursue them"

"It's kind of fun to do the impossible."

"First, think. Second, believe. And finally, dare."

"Why worry? If you've done the very best you can, worrying won't make it any better."

"Laughter is timeless, imagination has no age, dreams are forever."

Walt Disney died in 1966 but his legacy will live on forever. Positive messages from the Disney productions will continue to entertain and educate children and adults and continue to be seen in new Disney films that are produced following the same principles.

Again Walt Disney used the Positivity Principles throughout his life to dream big, believe in his vision and create changes to the world that are so much greater than the business itself.

Oprah Winfrey – Media

Rising from poverty in Mississippi, suffering abuse in childhood, Oprah Winfrey shows that your origins do not dictate your future. She is regarded as the most influential woman in the world, the 'Queen of All Media', the greatest black philanthropist in American history, and the richest African-American of the twentieth century. She became a millionaire by the age of 32, was worth $400 million at 41 years old, $2.9 billion by 60 years old. More importantly, she is ranked amongst the 'most admired women in the world', and one of the 'greatest Americans in the world'.

Oprah rose to fame with her unique talk show where she used compassion and empathy to help individuals unload their private lives to levels previously considered to be unachievable. She had a keen ability to relate to the suffering of others and help them find solutions, often giving her own money or connections to this end.

She continues to be an inspiration for others to become the best they can be, to overcome challenges in life, live with passion and enjoy every moment. She has a huge list of inspiration quotes that uplift and support people. "Passion is energy. Feel the power that comes from focusing on what excites you."

Oprah has openly supported minority groups and the disadvantaged. With her open support of tolerance to the LGBT groups on her show and in active debates, she has created a shift in understanding and acceptance of these groups around the world. "Excellence is the best deterrent to racism or sexism" and she proved this excelling in an industry where white, male presenters were the accepted norm.

Oprah is openly spiritual without intolerance of other groups. She started promoting a more openly spiritual message in the late 1990s with *Change Your Life* TV and took on the mantle of spiritual leader to her millions of followers. She also aired a program after the September 11 attacks called "Muslim 101" reflecting Islam's true peaceful nature and describing how it was the most misunderstood faith in the world.

By 2012, Oprah has given $400 million herself to educational causes; including $12 million in 2013 to the Smithsonian's National Museum of African American History and has raised millions of dollars to support needy causes through her program over the years. She has received multiple awards for her humanitarian acts and has been ranked amongst the most generous Americans in the past.

On the power of positive thought, she said:

"The greatest discovery of all is that a person can change his future by merely changing his attitude."

"Surround yourself only with people that will lift you higher."

"You become what you believe, not what you think or what you want."

"Don't let people talk you into what they think is you."

"Follow your instincts. That's where true wisdom manifests itself."

Reinforcing the principle of gratitude, she says: "The more you praise and celebrate your life, the more there is in life to celebrate".

"Be grateful for what you have; you'll end up having more. If you concentrate on what you don't have, you will never, ever have enough."

On the principle of aiming high, she says:

"The biggest adventure you can take, is to live the life of your dreams."

"Where there is no struggle, there is no strength."

"Whatever has happened to you in your past has no power over this present moment, because life in now."

Oprah Winfrey is a truly inspirational world leader, living Positivity Principles while spreading inspiration, love, hope and self-worth to millions of people around the world.

Summary

History keeps repeating the same story of individuals' phenomenal success, using passion, self-belief and a never give up attitude. They are generous people and share the keys to this success willingly. Who amongst us are going to use those proven principles to create share the podiums of success with these amazing people?

At any moment you can choose to use these principles to catapult your business into the same higher stratospheres of success – but what moment will you choose?

Epilogue

Spread the Positivity Message

These Positivity Principles will catapult you and your business to higher levels of success. The techniques work amazingly in business but are equally effective in everyday life, managing your personal matters, family, children and in every interaction you are going to have.

Our greatest joy is to teach people techniques that allow them to achieve success to levels that they never felt were possible. We know that remarkable changes in your life will occur when you put these processes in place. We still have surprisingly wonderful things happen that take our breath away, all because of these processes.

Spread the message of Positivity to every person in your circle of influence and the tsunami of goodwill will flow around you, through different groups and communities and this has the potential to make the world a better place!

Please share your stories with us through our websites and let others know how Positive Thinking and Positive Mindfulness Cognition has changed your workplace, success, business or personal lives.

We hope to see you enjoying your success and happiness in life. Enjoy the journey!

More information can be obtained from our websites and bookstores with training and support materials as well as free offers. Check it out at www.internationalpositivityinstitute.com

DR JOHN MCINTOSH &
REV ELIZABETH MCINTOSH
AUTHOR PROFILE

Authors, Entrepreneurs, Motivational
Speakers, & Humanitarians

John is an author, entrepreneur, medical doctor, motivational speaker and educator.

Elizabeth is an author, ordained minister, metaphysical scientist, motivational speaker, fitness trainer, yoga and meditation teacher, Reiki master, NLP practitioner, hypnotherapist, and life coach.

They are both motivational speakers and they write regular news columns, serve as television and radio presenters, and run seminars and retreats on self-development, business, health and wellbeing. Together, John and Elizabeth have produced a series of audio programs on health, relaxation and success, as well as a video documentary series. They are the proud winners of a wide variety of national and international literary, business, medical and management awards.

John has built multimillion dollar businesses in Australia and abroad using the philosophies and business principles that he shares in this books. His innovative thinking has empowered him to deliver medical services, set up health systems, and provide community education that combining traditional and complementary techniques for the best outcomes.

With his innovative approach using his medical skills to improve both staff productivity and wellbeing and the workplace culture, John has raised the standards of business management and is a recognised leader in his field.

Across many continents, John has also performed regular medical aid work being the team leader of expeditions to many remote islands as well as working selflessly locally and internationally in humanitarian roles.

In addition to building several multimillion dollar businesses in Australia and Indonesia, Elizabeth has been in clinical practice for many years. She brings together her broad-based skills and personal experiences that include international aid work and travel. The result is a unique fusion of modern Western science with ancient Eastern philosophies using the best of both worlds. As a keynote, corporate, and seminar presenter, she has shared innovative concepts that empower people to maximise their full potential.

After years of dealing with the consequences of negative thinking in their clinical practices, John and Elizabeth have crystallised the Positive Mindfulness Cognition™ technique. These techniques were explained in their first book *Mastering Negative Impulsive Thoughts,* winning literary awards. Their second book *CEO Principles* revolutionises the workplace with culture changing strategies, resulting in supportive, productive, and mentally resilient staff.

In their spare time, they enjoy sailing. John has competed in various sailing competitions on an international level.

They have both travelled and worked throughout Australia, Europe, United Kingdom, across Africa, Indonesia, the Americas and various South Pacific islands.

Dr John McIntosh & Rev Elizabeth are the co-authors of *CEO Principles* and live in Queensland, Australia.

RESOURCES

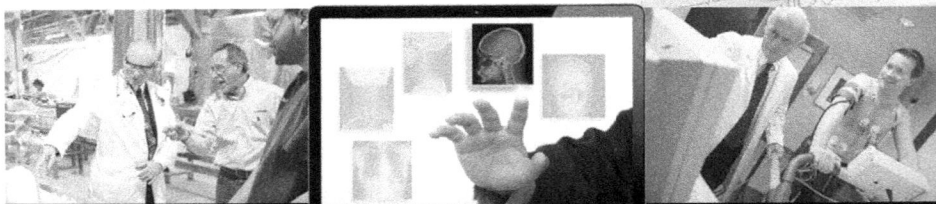

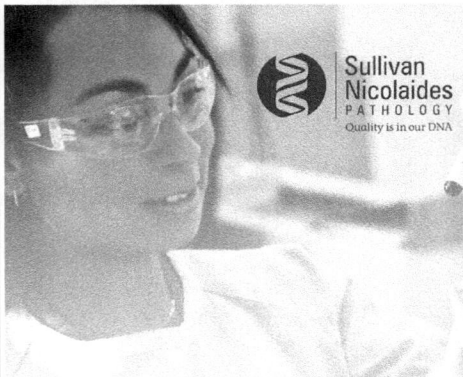

Neurophysics Therapy Institute

Over 30 years of research, producing phenomenal outcomes for hundreds of participants, the NeuroPhysics Therapy Institute's innovative exercise-based therapy is significantly contributing to the scientific understanding and treatment of complexities in disease, degeneration and optimisation of the human system; positively changing people's lives in the process.

Available for Rehabilitation, Performance Enhancement, Chronic Disorders and Complex Neurological Conditions

**NeuroPhysics Therapy Institute
Unit 5, 2 Energy Circuit
Robina, Gold Coast, QLD
(07) 5593 0688
www.neurophysictherapy.global**

NEUROPHYSICS
THERAPY
CLINIC